Revolutionary Desires

Published by 404 Ink Limited
www.404Ink.com
hello@404ink.com

Please note: Some references include URLs which may change or be unavailable
after publication of this book. All references within endnotes were accessible and
accurate as of January 2025 but may experience link rot from there on in.

Editing & proofreading: Heather McDaid
Typesetting: Laura Jones-Rivera
Cover design: Luke Bird
Co-founders and publishers of 404 Ink:
Heather McDaid & Laura Jones-Rivera

Print ISBN: 978-1-916637-08-5
Ebook ISBN: 978-1-916637-09-2

Printed and bound in Great Britain by Clays Ltd, Elcograf S.p.A.

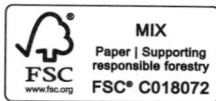

MIX
Paper | Supporting
responsible forestry
FSC® C018072

404 Ink acknowledges and is thankful for support from
Creative Scotland in the publication of this title.

LOTTERY FUNDED

Revolutionary Desires

The Political Power of the Sex Scene

Xuanlin Tham

Inklings

Contents

Introduction

In Luca Guadagnino's *Challengers*, there's a scene where Josh O'Connor's character Patrick, a young professional tennis player, dives into bed with his girlfriend, Tashi: he begins to kiss her stomach, lifting up her t-shirt with his teeth. Tashi, played by Zendaya, is a tennis prodigy biding her time at Stanford; Patrick is here to visit her while he's on tour. Their bodies are lithe, strong, beautiful, their youthful vitality emphasised by the unglamorous backdrop of an American college dorm room, that eternally recognisable space of sexual opportunity in the movies. Patrick's hands slip underneath Tashi's pink, see-through bra, and slide down to grab her ass; Tashi climbs on top of him, and when he rises up to meet her, she playfully, authoritatively pushes him back down. As important as the physical gestures here, though, is the verbal back-and-forth between their heated kisses and gropes: what, in their sport, you might call volleying. The scene is as much about physical desire as it is an

1

expression of the fact that to retain Tashi's attention, Patrick needs to stop being shit at tennis.

"You have no idea how lonely it is on tour," he says into her mouth while they kiss.

"Is that why you haven't won any Challengers?" she teases.

Tashi loves the game. She is exhilarated by the pleasures of being a high-performing tennis player, as well as the pleasures her body can bring her off the court. She is always looking for that sweet spot where desire makes playing the game better; where playing the game feels like that desire can be sublimated entirely. What Tashi wants, in many ways, is the centre of this film, and so is the fact that she's so, *so* hot that she ensnares two grown men into structuring their entire lives around her decade-spanning game of desire, tennis, and sex.

In short, the film is very sexy, and Tashi is very sexy. In a review that matches its subject's propulsive sexuality, IndieWire critic David Ehrlich writes that *Challengers* revels in "Zendaya's physical beauty", describing this scene as making "an IMAX-worthy spectacle of her ass, while another suggests that her raw sexuality is enough to whip up the biggest windstorm the tri-state area has seen since Hurricane Sandy."[1] Curiously, some deemed this language a masturbatory indulgence. This particular snippet drew reactions on social media like "Ehrlich wrote this shit with one hand", leading him to respond: "have the "anti sex scene" people graduated to being against the empirical fact of sexuality? these are straightforward descriptions of the framing in one scene, and how eroticism is expressed through the weather in another."[2]

The "anti sex scene" sentiment he refers to is largely centred around the idea that sex scenes are always unnecessary and gratuitous: they do not advance the plot, and have nothing of value to contribute to storytelling, characterisation, or any other composite attributes that tally up to make a film or TV show. Such utilitarian framing often seems to be working overtime to obscure a growing, deep-seated discomfort with sexuality that anxiously lies beneath the surface. Like many other things to do with sex – a topic that seems to fascinate and alarm us in equal measure, creating a paradoxical atmosphere where sex is both everywhere and something we must pretend doesn't exist – the sex scene has become a cultural talking point heavily invested with symbolic significance. In 2023, a study by the UCLA Centre for Scholars and Storytellers was widely covered by mainstream media for its headline-ready key finding that Gen Z want to see less sex on screen, while the ostensible importance of the age group being interviewed including ten-year-olds was largely ignored.[3] As with all "scandals", perhaps more important than the statistics themselves is how they might provide us with a legitimising terrain for a highly charged, acutely emotional debate. Every few months, some version of this conversation is impressively resuscitated by less and less provocative material; a veritable hydra of discourse, you may cut off its head, but two hundred tweets will emerge in its place. This phenomenon is striking, as despite increasingly commonplace protest against the sex scene, it is, in fact, disappearing: since the year 2000, the amount of sex and nudity in films has decreased by almost 40 percent.[4] What is it about sex and its representations that causes such a disproportionate reaction? And why should we care that the sex scene, by all measures, is vanishing off our screens?

For as long as the movies have existed, they've been talking about sex. It is not insignificant that one of the first films ever commercially screened to a public audience was Thomas Edison's *The Kiss* in 1896, an 18-second-long clip of stage actors May Irwin and John Rice locking lips; critics were apoplectic, calling the film "bestial" and "positively disgusting".[5] From the reign of the Hays Code, introduced in 1934 to combat 'obscenity' in Hollywood and forcing filmmakers like Alfred Hitchcock to imply sex on screen with a train entering a tunnel in *North by Northwest* (1959); to the international shock caused by unsimulated, hardcore sex in Nagisa Oshima's *In The Realm of the Senses* (1976), its undeveloped negatives shipped off to France to circumvent Japanese censors; and to pornography being the driving force behind why we have home video formats like VHS, DVD, and the streaming services we use today, the long history of the movies has, in many ways, been written by this push and pull: between our desire to get closer to sex via the moving image, and the social and legal regulation of what it should be allowed to reveal.

Today, the constantly recurring "debate" about the sex scene is a crucible within which we can see our ideas of sexuality shifting in real time. I talk about social media not to engage in terminally online navel-gazing, but because for better and for worse, the internet is perhaps the single most important realm today where sex itself is shaped. On some level, of course, there couldn't be anything further away from having sex than being on Twitter (I refuse to call it X, though the pornographic irony does not escape me). But sex is a discourse, in the incontrovertible fact that everything we understand about it – its norms, practices, imagery, gestures, associations, taboos – is shaped by how we talk about it. While we largely still think of sex as an intensely private act, to understand it as a discourse is to acknowledge the ways in which our most intimate behaviours and beliefs have been formed in dialogue with how sex is "spoken": drawing on Foucault, film scholar Linda Williams writes that we do not so much speak *about* sex, which "presumes a stable object of investigation", but *speak sex*, since "the very speaking forms part of sex's discursive construction."[6] Our idea of sex and sexuality, what it can and cannot be, is structured by a vast array of interconnected, material and ideological factors: everything from media platforms, gender socialisation, healthcare, housing, to the political and economic systems we live under – and of course, the movies.

Vanishingly few of us learn about sex the "proper way", if there is one. If the closest thing we have is sex education, its provision is nowhere near adequate, and its content can be dangerously dismal: sometimes, merely functioning as a thin veil for abstinence propaganda. Some of our very first encounters with sex and sexuality are thus likely to have arrived in the form of the moving image: whether it was the elusive implication of sex in a romantic film; a more explicit sex scene our parents might have fast forwarded through, grasping frantically for the TV remote; or, of course, pornography.

I don't know if I recall my first time watching sex on screen as a clearly-delineated event, but what I do remember from those early encounters is a haze of feelings, atmospheres, and illicitly enjoyed secrecies that for me, became inextricable from the process of falling in love with movies themselves. The prurience of flicking through the red-labelled 18s in the DVD section; secretly watching Todd Haynes' *Carol* when I was supposed to be doing homework, holding my breath as Cate Blanchett and Rooney Mara touched each other, bodies posed and framed like marble sculptures; and somewhere along the way, inheriting the shame that makes us embarrassed to talk and think about sex, let alone watch it, in front of other people. Today, I'm fascinated by that visceral response of discomfort, that imperative to look away. What might we find at its root?

I love a good sex scene. There's something about the particular way it reacquaints me with the immediacy of my body, whether I'm sitting in the movie theatre or slouched luxuriously in bed, laptop balanced on my thighs. We often say we are touched by a film, but what does this mean? Williams articulates how the sex scene in particular simultaneously "distances us from the immediate, proximate experience of touching and feeling with our own bodies" and "[brings] us back to feeling in these same bodies."[7] Some of the most important encounters with my identity and my desires have been granted to me by the sex scene, through the way it speaks to my body at the same time as my imagination, to proximity as well as distance: the distance that allows desire to exist. The sex scene can provide so much imagery, language and possibility where we have none; equally, it can capture the troubling ambivalences of sex, and make visible – even critique – the social, cultural, and political environment in which our most intimate acts and desires take shape. A good sex scene can allow us to get down, get messy.

What could it mean, then, to understand an increasingly popular opposition to the sex scene, one of the most culturally visible and powerfully immediate ways we "speak sex" into being, through an explicitly political lens? To think about our relationships to sex, art, and cinema as consumers under capitalism? What might emerge when we think about anti-sex scene sentiment amidst the rollback of reproductive rights, and its implied directive of abstinence; or the widespread, virulent attacks on our trans siblings? How might we think about the distance between our bodies and the bodies of others when homeless people and hotels full of asylum seekers are being set on fire? When horrific footage of genocide is livestreamed to our devices from Palestine, footage we are supposed to scroll past, never allow to permeate, so we move on like nothing is wrong? How do we contest the violence of deciding that some bodies do not matter, and that above all, our own bodies must remain unmoved and acquiescent? These threads are not as disparate as they initially seem. Exploring the sex scene as a political artefact can illuminate the myriad ways our bodies are being disciplined into action or inaction today.

Revolutionary Desires emerges from this moment, one that is both increasingly puritanical and increasingly violent, to make the case that far from being unnecessary, the sex scene is politically important. It intervenes with a staunch celebration of the power and necessity of sex on screen, not solely for the oft-cited reason that artistic freedom is important, but because of how cinema's erotic imagination – as a force that can shock, seduce, displace, overwhelm – can be politically transformative.

This book explores how our encounter with the sex scene can open up our bodies and minds to imagine the possibility of resistance to violent regimes of capitalism and patriarchy; how it can give us scripts for the kind of expansive, queer intimacies and solidarities that might help us build movements; how it could move us to demand real pleasure, which is also to demand liberation from a world that denies pleasure for so many. Desire reminds us that deep in our bones, there is something we want and don't have yet, and revolution has to be done by bodies that want to be free. Are you ready to fuck the system?

Chapter 1

The disappearance of the sex scene

On my walk home from work, I routinely make my way past a large LED billboard that feeds pedestrians and commuters a stream of advertisements: for eye serums, mobile phone plans, streaming services. Last year, I remember seeing one that read: 'Say hello to The Recliner. Buy online for £7.99.' From far away, it could have registered as an ad for an outrageously inexpensive armchair. Drawing slightly closer – or indeed, because of the familiar stylings of its black, white, and orange branding – you'd quickly realise it was an ad for the multiplex cinema chain, Vue.

I was struck by this ad: this idea that we could be enticed to the movie theatre not by what's on screen, but by the chairs we'd get to sit in. We are all very tired:

by work, care responsibilities, how the bare necessities of living, let alone leisure, are becoming unaffordable, perhaps tired of the uncomfortable sofa in a living room we will rent but never own. Maybe it's fine to show up for The Recliner's promise of structured comfort and distraction, and not really mind what we are being distracted by.

It is strange, though, that our bodies – beckoned towards The Recliner's business class plane seat mobility, the same bodies that keep this whole movie business afloat by buying tickets to watch something at the cinema – can be positioned at the forefront of the movie theatre experience, but are overwhelmingly becoming less of a concern for movies themselves. Cast an eye over the ads that plaster the sides of buses, what's steadily raked in billions at the box office over the past decade or so, and the way our theatres are becoming increasingly dominated by franchises, reboots, sequels and Cinematic Universes: do any of these films attempt to engage us meaningfully as bodies that touch, feel, desire?

Talking through his selections in the Criterion Collection's DVD closet, actor Gael García Bernal picks up a copy of Alfonso Cuarón's 2001 film *Y tu mamá también*. In this film, two teenage boys – one played by a then 21-year-old García Bernal – embark on a road trip across Mexico with a beautiful older woman. Together, with her guidance, they encounter lessons in love, friendship, grief, and life. Initially more of a horny, irreverent playground for the boys – the film's comedic opening scene sees them squeezing in one last quickie with their respective girlfriends before the girls catch a flight to Italy – sex is eventually where they shed their immature machismo in favour of discovering more profound intimacies, culminating with a devastatingly moving three-way that marks the film's bittersweet, vulnerable swan song. Sex is an essential part of the film's coming-of-age story, of the emotional textures of its characters' lives. Made over twenty years ago, the film feels like it belongs to a bygone era. "I want you to tell me which film has made you horny in the last years," García Bernal says, holding the DVD in his hands. "There's not many. I miss that from cinema."[8]

There is a particular travesty he identifies here. It's not just that the sex scene is becoming a rarity, but that the kind of film that's even interested in drawing us closer with touch, feeling, and visceral response – that eroticism itself, explicit or implied – is disappearing. Even beyond the remit of the erotic thriller and its heyday in the 1980s-90s, desire and sexuality was once regarded a normal topic of exploration across genres: as quotidian and worthy of attention as anything else in our lives. Mike Nichols' 1967 coming-of-age classic *The Graduate* had sex in it; Spike Lee's 1989 comedy drama *Do The Right Thing* had sex in it; even blockbusters and superhero movies contained some pretty unhinged sexual energy. Remember the ghost blowjob in *Ghostbusters*? Or Michelle Pfeiffer's iconic BDSM-inspired latex Catwoman costume in *Batman Returns*, and her lasciviously licking Michael Keaton's face?

Today, as culture congeals into an increasingly monolithic and corporatised shape, it's become harder to imagine that such broad and unremarkable space for sexuality once existed in our cinemas. In its place, a numbing distance has steadily grown between our bodies and those we see on screen. This is not because we've somehow ascended to some post-corporeal realm where the body is left behind: in her brilliant essay for *Blood Knife* Magazine 'Everyone is Beautiful and No One is Horny', writer Raquel S. Benedict traces how the physically "perfect" body – muscular, sculpted, flawless – has become the fetishised obsession of the movies, even as these same bodies are utterly drained of desire.[9] In the era of the superhero movie's unchallenged dominance over cinema, she astutely calls today's stars action *figures*, not action heroes. From Chris Evans' Captain America to Henry Cavill's Superman, they are homogenous, replicable, pristine, and ready to help us live out our fantasies of beating the shit out of the bad guys. They exist to be seen not so much as real human bodies, but as commodities: to sell you more of these movies. While those skin-tight costumes cling to every swell and crevice of muscle definition, there must remain an anxiously smooth lump where arousal and desire will never enter the frame. These bodies on screen are primed for violence, not sex. In Benedict's words, they are only horny for annihilation.

In 2021, the release of the superhero film *Eternals* – following the eponymous aliens secretly living on Earth who are forced to come out of hiding to protect it – sparked quite the commotion over the fact that it would contain the Marvel Cinematic Universe's first ever sex scene. Directed by Chloé Zhao, fresh from garnering the Academy Award for Best Director for her independent film *Nomadland*, *Eternals* saw Marvel attempt to position itself as capable of pivoting towards more arthouse sensibilities. Yet the much-talked-about sex scene (and the film itself) was comically slight and awkward. Following some incredibly chemistry-less kissing between Gemma Chan's Sersi and Richard Madden's Ikaris, two Eternals we are supposed to believe share a millennia-spanning romance, we cut to their disrobed bodies chastely rocking in missionary for about three seconds. It is a begrudging display of what Charles Pulliam-Moore, writing for *The Verge*, described as "perfunctory sexual congress".[10] The MCU had finally decided to confront the self-inscribed limits of its own sexlessness, yet found itself incapable of summoning even the slightest embodied desire needed to sell a sex scene between two beautiful people.

To play another Eternal named Kingo, actor Kumail Nanjiani underwent intense training to attain the unnaturally built physique now typical of the superhero film. According to Nanjiani's personal trainer Grant Roberts, although Zhao and Marvel were perfectly happy for Kingo to be "normal looking", the actor felt a certain responsibility to ensure that as a South Asian superhero, his character would be mega-ripped, too.[11] In an interview for *Men's Journal*, Roberts jokes about Nanjiani having the "softest core" he'd ever seen, saying he had no idea how the actor "was even able to stand up straight".[12] The training regimen consisted of "punishing" workout sessions five days a week for the year leading up to the shoot; intensive calorie restriction and meal planning; and the use of electric muscle stimulation, where you put on a suit of pads hooked up to wires that electrocute you every two to three seconds.[13] If this is what he'd put his body through, is it any wonder that the film's poor reception – described by critics as "puzzlingly bad", "numbing"[14], and "forgettable"[15] – left Nanjiani so shaken that he had to start going to therapy? "[My wife] Emily says I do have trauma from it," the actor shared on a podcast.[16]

"A body is no longer a holistic system," writes Benedict, exemplified by *Eternals'* curiously sexless sex scene and Nanjiani's gruelling pursuit of an inhuman, physical ideal (even more troubling for how explicitly its parameters are inscribed by whiteness). "It is not the vehicle through which we experience joy and pleasure during our brief time in the land of the living. It is not a home to live in and be happy. It is a collection of features: six pack, thigh gap, cum gutters. And these features exist not to make our lives more comfortable, but to increase the value of our assets."[17]

Reading Nanjiani's personal trainer joke about his "soft core" saddened me. Under late-stage capitalism, our bodies' disaggregation into its composite parts helps sell us the fantasy that our unhappiness might be remedied by consumerism, one generated insecurity at a time. Personal trainers and high-tech gym equipment, tummy slimming teas, push-up bras, jaw training gum, cellulite-melting creams. In a satirical video by animator Bryce Cohen posted to Instagram, a woman asks her date whether he thinks she's pretty: "What kind of pretty? Bunny pretty, deer pretty, rat pretty, frog pretty, girl pretty, boy pretty? I know I'm not quite 30 million likes pretty, but still pretty, right?"[18] The video's freneticism is exaggerated, but these are real things people say. In 1976, the psychoanalyst Erich Fromm wrote about the prevalence of 'the marketing character' – where one "experiences oneself as a commodity or, rather, simultaneously as the seller *and* the commodity to be sold."[19] In today's digitally mediated world – where every "social" platform is a marketplace – the mechanisms that underlie this phenomenon have only grown more sophisticated.

Once you believe you want to be 'bunny pretty', you can be convinced you should be buying these products, wearing these clothes, with your reward being the satisfaction of, in turn, getting to perpetuate this concept online. None of this will be out of an internally derived sense of satisfaction or pleasure, but because you have been enlisted into your own market segmentation.

As Ozempic sweeps across Hollywood, "heroin chic" becomes fashionable again, and the most widely-seen movies in the world flood our screens with body types only achievable through full-time personal training, calorie restriction, surgical procedures, taking steroids, or artificially suppressing your appetite, sex seems to be the last thing on our minds. "When a body receives fewer calories, it must prioritise essential life support systems over any function not strictly necessary for the body's immediate survival," Benedict writes. "Sexual desire falls into the latter category, as does high-level abstract thought. Is there anything more cruelly Puritanical than enshrining a sexual ideal that leaves a person unable to enjoy sex?"[20]

What is the significance of cinema being used to consolidate a monoculture of aesthetically, spiritually vacuous IP, unconcerned with the bodies of its stars or its audiences as things that can feel pleasure, especially sexual pleasure? What are we being lured into accepting, and what artistic, political, and agential possibilities are we being primed to foreclose? And how did we get here?

Today, the films seen as worth spending money to make and distribute are those marketable to the broadest of audiences, which therefore must include children. In an essay titled 'The Puritanical Eye: Hyper-mediation, Sex On Film, and the Disavowal of Desire', writer Carlee Gomes traces the disappearance of the sex scene alongside the shrinking space available for the now critically endangered mid-budget indie adult drama, where sex was simply, unremarkably depicted as part of life.[21] These films formed a healthy subset of mainstream cinema in the '90s: think *My Own Private Idaho*, the *Before* trilogy, or *The Talented Mr. Ripley*, whose star Matt Damon recently spoke about this very demise of the mid-budget film which used to be his "bread and butter".[22] Taking these films' place is the factory churn-out of the big budget, universally-sellable studio film: largely franchise-dominated and homogenous in content, aesthetic, and production, like those made for the Disney-owned MCU. In our post-9/11, American-dominated cinematic landscape, Gomes and Benedict also identify how it is movies that celebrate military strength, technology, and warfare – with unsurprisingly little room for community, connection, intimacy, or pleasure – which have proliferated and succeeded at the box office. If audiences for these films clamour for more mature content, this apparently means they want more graphic violence, never more sex. It is no coincidence that *Iron Man* was released in 2008, Gomes reminds us – just in time to bolster the American public's manufactured consent for the war in Iraq at its peak.

It's not just that our bodies are being configured by these movies as either weapons to be honed or collateral damage, instead of our lifelong home and a source of innate pleasure. It's also that if all the movies ask of us is to align ourselves with the good guys fighting the bad guys, our capacity to understand the very intimacies, vulnerability, messiness, and human complexity that makes sex possible is being eroded. Film theorist Vivian Sobchack writes about cinema being a fundamentally embodied experience, one we must literally make *sense* of to understand.[23] If both our bodies and our minds are held at a comfortable, unchallenging distance, if the movies no longer physically or intellectually engage us beyond the passive position of consumer, we lose this ability to make sense of sex, in both meanings of the word. Sex is becoming both unfeelable and unthinkable on screen. It is not just the sex scene itself that is vanishing, then: as Gomes writes, it's our "desire and literacy" for it, too.[24]

A lot of anti-sex scene sentiment thus revolves around the claim that the sex scene is unnecessary. Yet sometimes, the debate around the sex scene takes on an explicitly moralising character. In 2023, *You* actor Penn Badgley made headlines when he shared on his podcast that he no longer wished to film any intimate scenes.

"Fidelity in every relationship, including my marriage, is important to me," he said. "It's got to the point where I don't want to do that."[25] Though many found it odd how Badgley was equating performing simulated intimacy as an actor with cheating on his spouse – how were his co-stars supposed to feel about this revelation, for example? – I saw more than a few people (anecdotally, young women) applauding this conflation, such as a tweet claiming that Badgley's request "is the only thing that brings me hope for men today."[26] Binding the sex scene with the moral transgression of cheating on your wife is seen as the proper thing to do if you respect women, if you want to be a shining example for men, who are all dogs; conveniently, lambasting it provides an opportunity to shore up the moral goodness of the institution of heterosexual marriage and its monopoly on intimacy. In a 2019 interview, *Band of Brothers* actor Neal McDonough similarly said that he refuses to kiss anyone for a role because "these lips are meant for one woman", his wife.[27] Of course these actors are allowed to make their own decisions – but I'm interested in the meaning we, as publics, ascribe to these decisions. They are fascinating examples of a broader phenomenon: the sex scene's re-signification into a shameful vessel for the parts of us that are seen as base, ugly, and immoral.

Nowhere is this clearer than in the common retort that there's no need for the sex scene when pornography exists. It's perhaps useful to crudely sketch out some distinctions here – with the important acknowledgment that films can be pornographic and pornography can be cinematic, and that I do not believe the sex scene has to disavow porn, or claim to possess 'loftier' aims, to earn its right to exist. However, we might broadly agree that the purpose of pornography is to arouse the viewer and help bring them to orgasm, while the sex scene can have a much more diverse set of aims. Sex scenes can have a narrative purpose, communicating important information about character and storytelling; they can be funny, disturbing, sentimental, or dispassionate, eliciting a whole range of responses that can include arousal, but are not just limited to it. We might also agree that many of us feel alienated by most mainstream pornography, and are not turned on by the way it's framed as an exercise in maximising genital visibility or going harder and faster – and which, since its inception, has been largely inscribed around the heterosexual, cis male orgasm. Many of us might feel that movies tend to access a much richer variety, fluidity, and inventiveness when it comes to representing sex and desire, and thus, that they can feel more erotic to watch. When Linda Williams wrote that "sex is too important to be left to the porno-graphers",[28] she was not simplistically rallying against pornography, but saying that to do sex justice, to actually explore it as part of our physical and emotional lives,

21

will require much more imagination beyond its purely instrumental goals.

It's here where we can understand what truly lies beneath the instruction to just "go watch porn", couched in the language of 'go do it over *there*, not over here'. Porn is where we think sexuality can be quarantined and disposed of as no more than a transactional discharge. There is no need to confront the messiness of human relationality or experience in porn, where our position as the perfect, invisible voyeur is assumed and never challenged. This, to me, is one of the most important differences between pornography and the sex scene. In an age where we increasingly understand art through the lens of good guys and bad guys or 'problematic' and 'unproblematic', we no longer know what to make of the sex scene. Was it, or was it not, 'necessary'? Was it, or was it not, problematic? (Did Penn Badgley cheat, or not cheat, on his wife?) Can it be, as Gomes asks, "talked about in 240 characters", or "deciphered in the millisecond of a scroll?"[29] Is it even possible to speak about it on a social media platform like TikTok, where juvenile terms like "seggs", apparently used to avoid censorship, nevertheless reinforce the idea that sex is illicit and cannot be talked about openly?

In this line of thinking, sex and all its attendant irresolutions, ambiguities, excitements, and anxieties, should only ever be confined to porn: it shouldn't exist in the light of day, not in public, not in our movies. The directive to "go watch porn" – something already designated as private, taboo, yet ubiquitously accessible and therefore expedient – is an expression of the belief that sexuality can and should be cordoned off from our daily existence. And with it, the space that pleasure is allowed to take up in our lives and in our imaginations, the kind that's not tied to consumerism, grows smaller and smaller – until it is dulled and shamed out of us.

Why is this important? In her book *Pleasure Activism*, adrienne maree brown writes about what she's learned from supporting thousands of people as a coach, healer, doula, death doula, and facilitator: "I have seen, over and over … how denying our full, complex selves – denying our aliveness and our needs as living, sensual beings – increases the chance that we will be at odds with ourselves, our loved ones, our coworkers, and our neighbours on this planet."[30] Our deeply internalised acceptance of a status quo where we are denied time, space, and access to pleasure across our lives keeps us alienated, keeps us compliant. Because once we believe that intimacy, pleasure, and satisfaction outside of consumerism should be something we all have, and have in abundance, then the way the world is set up fundamentally must change.

We are a deeply immiserated and deprived population eking out survival under late-stage capitalism, an oppressive and violently unequal socioeconomic system in which many of us find it difficult to access the basic foundations of a safe and comfortable life – housing, food, adequate healthcare, to name a few – let alone intimacy. The case I wish to make is: it is important to make visible and displace the ossified determinacy of capitalism everywhere in our lives, especially in our bodies; to rediscover human connection amidst its rampant atomisation and dehumanisation; to fight for the health and transformative potential of our art against impoverished imaginations; to seek out intimacy in a world deprived of it; and that all these things are politically necessary to keep us ready, beating, alive, invested in and ready to fight for a future where joy, art, pleasure, and sex matters. I think the sex scene could help us get there.

In her seminal essay 'Uses of the Erotic', poet, philosopher, and activist Audre Lorde writes that every form of oppression depends on silencing those innate sources of power within the oppressed that might provide "energy for change". To Lorde, the erotic is one such suppressed source of power. "Our erotic knowledge empowers us, becomes a lens through which we scrutinise all aspects of our existence," she writes. "In touch with the erotic, I become less willing to accept powerlessness, or … resignation, despair, self-effacement, depression, self-denial."[31] What if the sex scene, as something that Williams describes as an artefact of "intertwined power-knowledge-pleasure",[32] could provide us with a way to become in touch with the erotic: a way to both recognise our immiseration and find the energy to refuse it? Tracing the sex scene's disappearance tells us an important story about the steady constriction of what we are allowed to imagine, feel, and experience under capitalist culture. Resurrecting it as an imaginative resource, as a portal to reconnecting with our bodies in a profoundly disembodying time, might seduce us into that most crucial first reawakening: the knowledge that we cannot settle for the world as it is today.

Chapter 2
The sex scene and capitalism

In a lush, jewel-toned strip club in downtown Toronto, a dancer named Christina performs the same routine night after night to Leonard Cohen's song 'Everybody Knows', while a tax auditor named Francis watches her in the audience. The choreography is magnetic: her movements methodical, weighed down by fatalism. With striking simplicity, Cohen's baritone narrates a collective experience of doomed circularity, the music's sticky-sweetness evoking the seductive catatonia we surrender to every day: "The poor stay poor, the rich get rich. That's how it goes."

We might initially assume that Francis is here for sexual titillation. Eventually, we discover that he is coping with immense personal tragedy, and has become compulsively dependent on a specific routine tied to this strip club. Every night, he pays Christina for a private dance, and talks to her, almost confessionally, while she strips. The financial transaction provides a guise for momentary intimacy, allowing something profound and strange to pass between the two of them – a ritualised exchange of sadness, trauma, and deep connection.

Atom Egoyan's 1994 film *Exotica* is a grief-stricken fairytale set against the backdrop of our alienation under late capitalism, where the consumerist promise of the strip club is itself stripped back, revealing something tender and wounded about how its characters' lives come to converge here. People slot their jagged shapes, ripped apart by loss and mourning and unspeakable need, into the infrastructure of the club, and the machine keeps running. Among many of the breathtaking things the film illuminates is the fact that our intimate, sexual, and affective lives have become increasingly unintelligible and unliveable outside the framework of a transaction. Thirty years later, this observation is even more acute: the prevailing answer to the distress of everyday life is to pay for therapy, even though the fact that more of us are mentally ill than ever before should be seen as an alarming structural failure; time with friends, romantic, or sexual partners continues to be taken out of a zero-sum equation with the work that pays for our survival; our emotional energy is increasingly funnelled into social media, where the promise of "connection" leaves us disconnected and disembodied but nevertheless unable to leave, and our dutiful scrolling lines the pockets of tech companies and advertisers.

The easy infiltration of the workings of capital into the most intimate details of human life – to say nothing of the macro violences wrought by climate catastrophe or the global military industrial complex – means the slogan "it is easier to imagine the end of the world than the end of capitalism" has only gained in salience. Popularised by Mark Fisher, who attributes its formulation to Slavoj Žižek and Fredric Jameson, this slogan is the essence of Fisher's concept of capitalist realism: "the widespread sense that not only is capitalism the only viable political and economic system, but also that it is now impossible even to *imagine* a coherent alternative to it."[33]

Since the 1980s, the decade when Margaret Thatcher infamously declared "there is no alternative", capitalism has so successfully installed itself as the natural order that its provisional dominance has become invisible. Yet as anthropologist David Graeber reminds us, drawing on Marxist philosopher John Holloway, it "only exists because every day we wake up and continue to produce it".[34] The "ultimate revolutionary question" might be: "what are the conditions that would have to exist to enable us to do this – to just wake up and imagine and produce something else?"[35]

If culture is essential in shaping our imaginations, what lies in its immense pool of images and discourses that could be harnessed to catalyse this kind of break in capitalism's looping continuity? Political theorist Mihaela Mihai writes about how art, with its uniquely mediated and pleasurable nature, can be a safe, accessible way to explore dissenting from institutionally entrenched, dominant scripts that purposefully limit our political imagination. She identifies how simple "awareness raising" is insufficient to dislodge our emotional and embodied investments in dominant political mythologies: what is needed is some element of seductive sabotage.[36] Her use of seduction as a metaphor is all too fitting; the sex scene might be just the saboteur we need. One of the most visceral ways an art form can instantaneously bring us back to sensing in our bodies (just think about the blood rush it instigates, maybe the held breath; the heightened awareness of other people in the room, the way you might begin to feel your clothes against your skin), the sex scene is, by nature, an interruption: a moment of pause in the otherwise smooth automatism of our disembodied media consumption. Where the experience of watching a film is often understood as a passive absorption, Linda Williams writes that "the shock of eros" decisively transforms this encounter into a "two-way street: our bodies both take in sensation and then reverse the energy of that reception", becoming

29

activated as what film historian Miriam Hansen describes as a "porous interface between the organism and the world."[37]

Many of us know that capitalism is hellish; in fact, being able to express this very sentiment has become a way of allowing ourselves to be reassimilated, frictionless, into its continued existence. Fisher suggests this is why a moral critique of capitalism has failed to generate any significant opposition, and instead reinforced the conviction that no alternative exists. "Poverty, famine and war can be presented as an inevitable part of reality, while the hope that these forms of suffering could be eliminated easily painted as naive utopianism," he writes.[38] What is needed is a glitch in the surface: for the porous interface of our bodies to become receptive to the fact that 'reality' under capitalism remains contingent, up for grabs.

Let us examine three ways in which the sex scene can sabotage capitalist mythologies: first, by confronting us with the commodification of sex; second, by utilising the "shock of ėros" to make the invisibilised atmosphere of capitalist realism visible; and finally, by flooding our senses with the erotic energy to break past it and power collective visions of pleasure, which is to say, collective visions of what lies beyond.

As a kind of cultural archive that insists upon sex as a part of human life, the cinematic sex scene can, by sheer fact of its presence, alert us to the shrinking time and space available for pleasure that capitalism allows for our daily existence. Certain films go further: like *Exotica*, set within the explicitly capitalist infrastructure of the strip club, or Paul Verhoeven's *Showgirls*, which follows a dancer named Nomi Malone and her cutthroat journey to stardom as a Vegas showgirl. Both films lay bare the fact that everything is a market under capitalism, and foreground the exploitative relations that funnel profits from sex work upwards. As we watch Christina give Francis a lapdance in *Exotica*, or see Nomi athletically fucking her boss in *Showgirls*, we are asked to confront our own complicity in the commodification of sex as voyeur-consumers of these films, too. While sex work might be the most materially immediate realm where market forces structure our intimate acts, these scenes remind us that the commodification of sex – for example, in the movies – stretches far beyond it.

This is certainly the case made by sexual economics theory, an outdated yet fascinatingly blunt proposition that sex has a market price: here, women gatekeep access to sex, and men compete with each other to buy it with non-sexual resources.[39] Applying basic laws of supply and demand, when male demand for sex exceeds women's supply of it, the price of sex is high, meaning women can bargain for more in exchange for sex; inversely, when women's supply of sex exceeds its demand from men, the price of sex is low, meaning men can buy access to women's sexuality for less. Proposed by psychologists Roy Baumeister and Kathleen Vohs in the 2000s, it's the kind of heteronormative, gender essentialist 'men are from Mars and women are from Venus' drivel we might easily dismiss now. Yet this impulse to theorise sexuality as a market is itself worth examining, revealing a willingness to assume that human interaction is, by nature, transactional.

In *Showgirls*, sex explicitly plays out in terms of a transaction: whether it's money that changes hands, status, or power. Sex is not just sold on stage; rather, *Showgirls* demonstrates how the capitalist logic that commodifies bodies comes to define all human interaction. Nomi has hitchhiked to Vegas with her dreams of stardom, crashing on a friend's couch and dancing at a nightclub to make ends meet. But Cristal Conners, star of the 'Goddess' show at the Stardust casino, angers her by saying Nomi is a prostitute, not a performer. When Cristal and her boyfriend Zack, the entertainment director at the Stardust, visit Nomi at the club, she is nevertheless unable to refuse the $500 Cristal pays her to give Zack a private lapdance. Buying Nomi's body and her dignity is a power trip for Cristal, but Nomi gets her own back: holding intense eye contact with Cristal as she gyrates propulsively on Zack's lap, she makes him come in his pants.

Sex (with Zack) becomes a game of one-upmanship between them, with an explicitly material, economic result. To secure her place as Cristal's understudy at the Stardust, Nomi has sex with Zack in the neon-lit swimming pool of his ostentatious Vegas mansion. In what has become *Showgirls'* most infamous scene, and the pinnacle of what the film's detractors call bad taste, Nomi thrashes around on Zack in the pool with the freneticism of the earlier lapdance and then some: her upper body flailing so violently as they fuck that her head disappears under water, and all we can see of her is a naked, gleaming torso. While critics lambast the ridiculousness of this sex scene, the lurid, exaggerated unpleasantness of watching Nomi enthusiastically participate in her own dehumanisation is clearly not supposed to be sexy. She is a showgirl; she has to perform. The film seems to ask us: what happens when sex is no longer about pleasure, but providing the spectacle The Man paid for, in exchange for material security? When it is a commodity that only attains value in an exchange, and only ever a means to an end? *Showgirls'* mode of excess merely amplifies the often invisibilised dynamics of sexual economics to graphic extremity: in our forced confrontation with how the logic of capitalism has fully colonised Nomi's intimate life, its artificial, violent imposition becomes glaringly obvious.

Sexual economics theory should not, however, be understood as a descriptive theory for gender or human nature, but as contingent on capitalism. In *Why Women Have Better Sex Under Socialism*, anthropologist Kristen Ghodsee surveys sociological research suggesting that women experienced higher levels of sexual satisfaction in socialist states than capitalist states: a comparative study of East and West Germany, for example, found that East German women had a higher rate of orgasm than West German women.[40] She examines how a confluence of factors helped decouple sexual intimacy from economic considerations in socialist states, possibly contributing to this greater level of sexual fulfilment: women's employment and financial autonomy meaning they could choose sexual partners based on compatibility, attraction, and desire; or state initiatives socialising the unpaid reproductive labour borne by women (childcare, laundry, cooking) freeing up time for adults to nurture intimate relationships. While sexual economics theory rests on assumptions that appear both misogynistic and simplistic to the point of inaccuracy, Ghodsee points out that its very reductionism "gives valuable insight into the way sexuality is experienced in capitalist societies" specifically: "Essentially, sexual economics theory is right, but only within the confines of the free market system."[41] A similar explanatory bluntness, I argue, lends a film like *Showgirls* its critical power too: to illuminate, unsparingly, the reduction of sexuality into crude exchange under the infrastructure of capitalism.

Yet the commodifying logic of capitalism can not only be revealed within the dynamics of a sex scene, but the manner in which we talk about the sex scene itself. Recall the common refrain that sex scenes are "unnecessary". Unnecessary for what? Does sex need to have a purpose? This idea that the sex scene should be instrumental, productive somehow, is internalised capitalism par excellence. Pleasure for pleasure's sake has become unthinkable. Everything must have a narrowly defined *purpose*: it must be legible and contained within the marketable, commodifiable mechanism of plot; it must bolster capital exchange in some form, if only by permitting consumers to digest it with ease. The anxious need to disavow the pornographic seems to haunt this sentiment, too: sex for its own sake is not only valueless, but terrifying somehow, which speaks of a learned suspicion of bodily pleasure that serves capital accumulation.

During a test screening for David Cronenberg's 1996 film *Crash,* an audience member fed back to the director that "a series of sex scenes is not a plot". Cronenberg recalls in an interview: "I said, 'Why not? Who says?' And the answer is that it can be, but not when the sex scenes are the normal kind of sex scenes: lyrical little interludes and then on with the real movie."[42] A chrome-cold, erotic odyssey, *Crash* follows a married couple who fall in with a group of car crash fetishists seeking ever-greater sexual thrills from reenacting famous car crashes, fucking in moving or wrecked cars, colliding with each other on the roads, watching crash test footage, and ruminating on the violent fusion between flesh and metal as they pursue every possible little death – *petite mort* – on the precipice of the final one. Released to great controversy with a NC-17 rating, and the subject of a moral panic that led to a (mostly unsuccessful) campaign to ban its theatrical release in the UK,[43] *Crash* is a visceral literalisation of the violences of late-stage capitalism and its derealising impact on our bodies and psyches. Harnessing the initial, concussive dissonance of the idea that a car crash could ignite sexual arousal, *Crash* pierces through the dazed automatism of mundane life, forcing *the* fetish object of consumerism, the automobile, to become foreign and dangerous to us once more.

"A car is not the highest of high tech," Cronenberg says. "But it has affected us and changed us more than anything else in the last hundred years. We have incorporated it. The weird privacy in public that it gives us."[44] The archetypal product of industrialised capitalism, the car represents our grand retreat into privatisation: a way of life socioeconomically structured around the atomised individual. Brutally warping capital's promise of safety, ease, happiness, and fulfilment like a sheet of metal, *Crash* confronts us with the distorted reflection of capitalist realism: suppressed knowledge of widespread alienation and disillusion; libido sublimated into inanimate objects, as if taking the logic of consumerism to its final, perverse extreme; and omnipresent violence waiting to puncture the surface.

Crash feels "peculiarly American",[45] to quote critics Mikita Brottman and Christopher Sharrett, even though it is based on the eponymous British novel by J.G. Ballard and directed by a Canadian filmmaker. Its landscape feels archetypically capitalist in its desolation, its narrative dealing with "the exhaustion of the civilising process, and of the final expenditures of the horizontal, forward-moving momentum that drove this enterprise."[46] Cronenberg's derelict vision of Toronto, all industrial concrete buildings and anonymous, vacant spaces, feels haunted by a promise of modernity that has come and gone. The film drives us through the wasteland of the 'end of history': American political scientist Francis Fukuyama's 1989 claim that following the collapse of the Soviet Union, Western liberal democracy and market capitalism was "the endpoint of mankind's ideological evolution".[47]

Crash spins around this endpoint with a futureless circularity. Repeatedly failing to orgasm, its central couple whispers to each other, "maybe the next one", their episodic pursuit of pleasure not unlike the compulsive recursion of consumerism, where true satisfaction must always elude capture. Materially, however, the sex in this film is entirely antithetical to the reproduction of capital:

it seeks to destroy both body and property; pleasure ad infinitum is the point, not subsumed under some other 'constructive' purpose; and it is explicitly anti-reproductive. The sexual vignettes that make up *Crash* are nearly all masturbatory, anal, homosexual, or configured around a new, cyborg erogenous zone – such as the vulva-like leg scar of a car crash survivor, bracketed by stiff metal braces. Brottman and Sharrett suggest that the film's transgressive, taboo anality – and I add, its fixation on all other non-reproductive orifices and surfaces, including those of the car – is a sexual pun for the "dead end of human experience", a defiant, degenerate attitude towards human life.[48] *Crash*, one surmises, does not give a shit about reproducing the workforce.

Watching it, one is overcome with a sense of unease at its coolness, its quiet: its characters' voices never quite rise above a dispassionate murmur even during sex, and the lethal violence that hurls their bodies off highways is met with no more than itching curiosity and tempered arousal. Chris Rodley, the editor of *Cronenberg on Cronenberg*, writes that *Crash* disorients precisely because of its "refusal to get too excited": "unable to seek refuge in the delirium of a fever, the viewer is therefore consigned to an unsettling state of total awareness in the face of delirious behaviour".[49] *Crash* mirrors our collective desensitisation to pathological violence that perpetuates capitalism's continued survival. Responding to Fukuyama's 'end of history' in words that have only grown horrifically more apt since 1993, philosopher Jacques Derrida wrote: "At a time when some have the audacity to neo-evangelise in the name of an ideal of liberal democracy: never have violence, inequality, exclusion, famine, and thus economic oppression affected as many human beings in the history of the earth ... let us never neglect this evident macroscopic fact, made up of innumerable singular sites of suffering".[50]

Crash mobilises the bodily shock of eros, the visceral interruption of the transgressive sex scene, to confront us with the incredible everyday violence of capitalist realism and its seamless integration into our idea of normalcy. "The most Gothic description of Capital is also the most accurate," Fisher writes. "Capital is an abstract parasite, an insatiable vampire and zombie-maker; but the living flesh it converts into dead labour is ours, and the zombies it makes are us."[51] Observing its characters with a detached uninterest in passing moral judgement on their actions, *Crash* evades definitive interpretation: are its 'zombies' simply meandering towards annihilation, or have they, by virtue of incorporating capitalism's violence for their pleasure, carved out something strangely utopian? The group's cult of personality ringleader, Vaughan, certainly thinks the latter: speaking reverently of the car crash as a "benevolent psychopathology that beckons towards us", he believes the next step in our evolution lies in embracing the brutal fusion of body and technology.

Despite *Crash*'s breathtakingly innovative sexual experimentation, Brottman and Sharrett suggest that "the notion of the car crash - and sexual pathologies in general - as liberatory seems undercut by the gloom of the film",[52] particularly given its ending: husband and wife, having almost killed each other in a crash, begin to fuck once more in the wreckage, murmuring "maybe the next one" as the screen fades to black. If *Crash*'s characters do not seem truly liberated yet, perhaps it is because the scale of their insurrection feels necessarily limited: their efforts too inward-looking to harness enough momentum to break out of the fatalistic cycle of capitalism. In its negativity, however, the film reveals to us precisely the "crashed present" of capitalist destruction: the "ideo-logical rubble" from which new realities can take hold.[53] But for that, we need a revolutionary movement.

The French philosopher Georges Bataille once defined eroticism as "assenting to life up to the point of death."[54] In other words, eroticism is a realm where we can momen-tarily suspend our avoidance of pain, fear, and loss in the pursuit of even greater pleasure – where the borders of the self expand to accommodate something bigger. Could this not be an energetic source for revolutionary politics? *The Matrix Reloaded* says yes. In this sequel to 1999's *The Matrix* – perhaps the most influential science fiction blockbuster of all time, and one of the greatest anticapitalist critiques ever contained within a genre film – Zion, the underground city of humans freed from the Matrix, has just been informed that within 24 hours, a machine army intent on annihilating them will reach the city. Resistance leader Morpheus addresses Zion:

I remember that for one hundred years we have fought these machines. I remember that for one hundred years they have sent their armies to destroy us. And after a century of war, I remember that which matters most: we are still here!

The crowd of thousands roars with strength, roused by the power of his conviction:

Let us send a message to that army. Tonight, let us shake this cave. Tonight, let us tremble these halls of earth, steel, and stone; let us be heard from red core to black sky. Tonight, let us make them remember: *this is Zion, and we are not afraid!*

Drums begin to beat; bare feet stamp the ground; Zion starts to dance. Our protagonist Neo and his fellow fighter and lover, Trinity, find each other in the crowd. They escape to their room, seizing the opportunity to finally be alone. Acoustic drumming gradually builds to a beat drop, and the city begins to rave to the sound of techno; if the origin of the rave is a defiant, illegal occupation of space, what could be more fitting for Zion – a queer, trans underworld of freed bodies that rebel against enslavement by the machines – on the eve of this revolutionary battle? The camera pans across sweaty bodies in slow-mo, luxuriating over gleaming skin on skin, before cutting to Neo and Trinity having sex; then we cut back to the rave and its grinding bodies, hands gripping thighs, nipples pressed against mesh clothing. The music pulses euphorically as we alternate between Neo and Trinity and the rave, connecting all of Zion in a heady wavelength of embodied, ecstatic pleasure. There is a profound sense that the erotic is political in this moment – that the affirmation of human desire, connection, and sexuality is absolutely essential to Zion's survival. The sex scene ends with a shot of Neo and Trinity embracing, with Neo's back to us: as the camera zooms out, it is as if their bodies have melded together, and the individual has dissolved. It is a precursor to what an exiled computer program named the Keymaker will tell them about their mission later in the film, upon which all of humanity depends: "All must be done as one. If one fails, all fail."

Reading Audre Lorde, academic Nikki Young writes: "By resurrecting the power of the erotic, Lorde affirms our simultaneity as selves who exist in individual potentiality and selves whose connectivity is based on the freedoms of our sensuality."[55] *The Matrix Reloaded* posits exactly this idea – that eroticism is at once a rooting into the power of the self and a radically connective force that extends outwards, allowing us to sense our belonging to a collective. In the sensate euphoria of Neo and Trinity fucking while their fellow resistance fighters rave through the night, we find a beautiful expression of revolutionary eroticism, and the essence of what it means to "dissent": trans academic Cael M. Keegan elaborates this as literally meaning to "differ in sentiment", to "sense not what others sense, but something else."[56] In Zion's mass of dissenting bodies, eroticism is a forward-looking vision: it proclaims, with every sensation, what their fight for liberation is for. They sense that a future of freedom and pleasure is not only possible, but necessary.

This scene in *The Matrix Reloaded* won a Guardian poll for the worst sex scene of all time.[57] *Reloaded*, however, deserves to be considered one of the most radical sequels ever made for how much it circumvented audience expectation, including with this bold, lengthy sex scene. Today, the sequel or reboot has become the primary mode of cinematic narrativity, generating profit from our attachment to the familiar: a mode reflective of the cyclical futurelessness of our present, and our inability to imagine new political formations. Our screens are replete with a litany of *Fast and Furious*es, live-action remakes of

The Lion King, and edgy takes on Batman villains, as if we are only allowed to want what we have seen before. Yet the *Matrix* sequels refuse to merely extend the familiar, even at the cost of alienating their audiences. Radically undermining Neo's straightforward hero's journey in the first film in favour of the collectivist vision of Zion as revolutionary movement, *Reloaded* does not just perform a narrative subversion, but a critique of studio film-making's self-cannibalising ecosystem.

As *Reloaded* approaches its final act, we learn that the prophecy of Neo as The One, humanity's saviour figure, is merely another system of control. There have been five Ones before Neo, and all have been faced with the same choice of two doors: one door initiates the routine reloading of the simulation, after which a few humans can be extracted to rebuild Zion; the other door leads back to the Matrix (where Trinity is currently bleeding out from a gunshot wound) and kills everyone connected to it. Neo's predecessors have always chosen the first door, but it is his erotic, sensual, and romantic relation to Trinity that allows him to make the unthinkable choice of walking through the other door. Instead of accepting the cruelty of being forced to weigh Trinity's survival against that of humanity, Neo is determined to reject both outcomes: triggering a series of events that will – after enormous sacrifice, including Neo's own martyring for the cause – break humanity out of this cycle of oppression.

Neo's refusal to accept the parameters of choice forced upon him is a beautifully instructive revolutionary impulse for this moment in time, where electoral politics have seemingly foreclosed all political imagination beyond a horrifying comparative exercise to determine 'the lesser of two evils'. (Reproductive healthcare and genocidal imperialism, or no reproductive healthcare and genocidal imperialism?) Fisher writes that "to reclaim a real political agency means first of all accepting our insertion *at the level of desire* in the remorseless meat-grinder of Capital"[58] – in other words, nothing could be more urgent than recognising how our political 'choices' have been programmed to cause minimal threat to the infrastructure of our oppression. We need to revolutionise desire: to use it as a way to look ecstatically beyond the choices prescribed to us. Far from being a cliche romance plot, Neo and Trinity's love and sexual connection is thus essential to *Reloaded*'s revolutionary politics. Co-director Lana Wachowski, in an interview with Keegan, said:

It was not easy to put sex in the trilogy, but I needed it … We did not want [Neo and Trinity's] relationship to be like so many relationships we see today in film, without physical, sexually mature connection. I needed to understand Zion as *bodies*, and if you want to understand bodies, you have to understand *desire*. The condition of identity – if that's your investigation – the human condition, you can't *not* talk about sex.[59]

To Italian philosopher Franco 'Bifo' Berardi, the social excitement of revolution is indistinguishable from erotic excitement: the "pleasure of a crowd", how we overcome political despair together as a collective of bodies, is what powers a movement.[60] Desire is not an insular experience. It is not just to "crave" someone or their body, but to "imagine a situation where [...] we are the same thing, the same event."[61] It is this fusion of possibilities, this radical re-making of reality to choose oneself, one's lover, and one's political desires all at the same time, that drives Neo's revolutionary act.

From the rubble of the crashed present, then, where bodies, choices, and narratives are constrained by the dehumanising logic of capitalism, emerges the erotic as a source of wild possibility: something that connects my body to your body, to all our bodies, allowing us to break out of the circularity of the present and sense a future beyond it. The erotic energy of the sex scene might both instigate a necessary interruption of our automated drift through capitalist time, and provide us with the imaginative, embodied momentum to demand revolution.

Chapter 3
The sex scene under patriarchy

In 1972, a film called *Deep Throat* was released in American cinemas and became one of the first and most successful feature-length, hard-core pornographic films to enter the mainstream. It was synonymous with a short-lived era that came to be known as 'porno chic': where watching porn in the cinema, with other people, was deemed part of one's cultural duty. *Deep Throat* follows a woman – played by Linda Boreman, stage name Linda Lovelace – on a quest for an elusive orgasm: when her doctor discovers her clitoris is in fact located in her throat, he tells her that deep-throat fellatio is the solution to her sexual woes. Delighted, she experiments with fellating several patients until she finds one who can satisfactorily hit the spot, and marries him.

Part of the wider cultural landscape of the sexual revolution, *Deep Throat* nevertheless came to represent more troubling things. With its central premise being a fictionally located clitoris, it visually and narratively allowed the 'money shot' of a woman's face next to an ejaculating penis to upstage an otherwise "invisible" female pleasure in mainstream, filmed sex.[62] This failure to attribute importance to sexual acts or sensations which were not readily visible – in other words, the cumshot's availability to the camera as opposed to the 'invisible' pleasure of the vagina or clitoris – would become the very language of pornography itself.

While Boreman wrote a pornographic memoir soon after the film's release that described it as a liberating experience, eight years later, she revealed that she had been forced into prostitution and pornography by her abusive manager and husband, Chuck Traynor, and coerced into performing the sex acts in *Deep Throat*.[63] She testified in 1986: "Virtually every time someone watches that movie, they're watching me being raped." In its commodification of these images, *Deep Throat* could be thought of as a watershed event wherein, despite the optimistic disobedience of the 'sexual revolution', the movies were recruited to affirm public and dominant understandings of sexuality in service of capitalism and one of its main disciplining forces: patriarchy.

The cultural disciplining of female sexuality has always been essential to reproduce capitalism: to maintain the viability of the nuclear family; to offer women's bodies, labour, and emotional and sexual lives to their husbands as refuge from the ills of work; to make sure a man's private property would be passed down to legitimate heirs produced by monogamous marriage; and to ensure, as President Richard Nixon basically decreed in 1971 when he vetoed the funding of a national child care system, that the government should never pay for anything that women could just do for free.[64] Patriarchy is thus not just congenial to neoliberal capitalism, but essential for its existence. While a hard-core porno about a woman who conveniently discovers she loves giving blowjobs doesn't seem, at first blush, to chime with Nixon's conservative 'family values', in a way, *Deep Throat* very much did. Under the banner of sexual liberation, it underscored existing dynamics of patriarchal oppression by eroticising and commodifying the submission of women's sexuality to men. This, surely, remains one of the most serious charges against the sex scene: that its visual language reinforces women's social and sexual inequality; and at worst, that it sells us tickets to watch a woman being coerced into performing sex for the camera.

Three years after *Deep Throat*, film theorist Laura Mulvey would publish her landmark essay *Visual Pleasure and Narrative Cinema*. Mulvey argued that mainstream Hollywood cinema had "coded the erotic into the language of the dominant patriarchal order", which structured how we looked at and derived pleasure from film itself.[65] A work of psychoanalytic criticism, the essay contends that the cinematic modes of voyeurism (woman as mystery to be solved) and fetishism (woman objectified, so she becomes reassuring) were developed to overcome the castration anxiety of the male spectator. But the psychoanalysis has largely taken a backseat to the concept most people now associate with Mulvey: the "male gaze". She writes:

> In a world ordered by sexual imbalance, pleasure in looking has been split between active/male and passive/female. The determining male gaze projects its phantasy on to the female figure ... women are simultaneously looked at and displayed, with their appearance coded for strong visual and erotic impact so that they can be said to connote *to-be-looked-at-ness*. Women displayed as sexual object is the leitmotif of erotic spectacle ... she holds the look, plays to and signifies male desire.[66]

Since *Visual Pleasure*, the concept of the "male gaze" has been widely enlisted in describing women being posed for men's erotic pleasure on screen: oft-cited examples include Margot Robbie in *Wolf of Wall Street*, letting Leonardo DiCaprio stare up her skirt while she holds his face back with her stiletto; the metal bikini

Carrie Fisher wears as Princess Leia in *Return of the Jedi*; or Megan Fox arching her back as she looks under the hood of a car in *Transformers*. Today, the sex scene is often criticised as being pure fodder for this male gaze: the ultimate mechanism of women's objectification for the camera.

Invoked as its empowering antidote is the concept of the "female gaze": which has become shorthand for the idea that female filmmakers naturally transcend the patriarchal norms of mainstream cinema, and that a woman behind the camera is inherently radical. Critic Emily Nussbaum writes that this concept has "become blunt from overuse, particularly with its essentialist hint that women share one eye: a vision that is circular, mucky, menstrual, intimate, wise."[67] We should be suspicious of how this is often used to close ranks around a specific expression of femininity – one that is largely white, suspicious of sexuality, and aimed at cis women. Yet beyond the question of whether this homogenising, yonic eye makes for good art, it also just clearly doesn't exist. In French filmmaker Coralie Fargeat's much-lauded 2024 'feminist' body horror *The Substance*, a bluntly cautionary tale about how it's a bad idea to internalise Hollywood's male gaze and its objectifying, ageist beauty standards, the camera repeatedly positions Margaret Qualley's ass in the middle of the frame: plump and youthful, it's there to be lusted over, and not just by the creepy studio execs in the film, but by us. Some might argue that this is merely an externalisation of how Qualley's character feels, which is young and hot and fuckable – but is this the "female gaze" at work? Does Fargeat not also, in Mulvey's words, "neatly combine" the erotic "spectacle" of a woman's body and "narrative"? In assigning utmost importance to who the gaze belongs to, do we absolve ourselves of interrogating what we are being asked to look at, and how?

There is a likely reason that the concept of these gendered gazes continues to occupy such a foremost place in our vocabulary: it promises simplicity. The 'male gaze' allows us to distil everything troubling about the mechanics of patriarchy, behind and in front of the camera, to a single point. It's easy to see why the sex scene, construed as the male gaze at its most extreme, has become a particular symbol of this, especially given that the greatest contemporary reckoning with the sexual violence of patriarchy began with Hollywood itself. #MeToo and Harvey Weinstein taught us that sexual violence is not only ubiquitous but also, as with *Deep Throat*, potentially immortalised on screen; the sheer scale of (ongoing) allegations against powerful men in the industry makes the very infrastructure of mainstream filmmaking seem inextricable from it. Part of the effect these revelations have had is an increased concern and vigilance about what art is okay and what is "problematic" – a judgement often levied at the sex scene, perhaps because it summons too proximately the sexual harassment, coercion, and subjugation of women we know happens off-screen. I sympathise with this greatly, but wish to question why our goodwill and broad desire for justice now largely takes the form of deciding what to consume. As we are increasingly stripped of any meaningful political and civic agency, perhaps the final realm in our lives we have some semblance of control over is what we buy. In such a scenario, the act of engaging with media acquires heightened, moralistic proportions: what we consume "must be perfectly virtuous, sanitised of all problematic or complicated ideas and depictions, because it has become the stand-in for ... our very political action as citizens," says writer Carlee Gomes.[68] When all other avenues feel closed off, we begin to view consumption as not only a political act, but *the* political act.

What's lost when this happens? During the feminist sex wars of the 1980s, some pro-porn feminists wrote that those on the other side of the debate found it easier to "attack the picture of what oppresses us than the mysterious, elusive ... thing itself".[69] The sex scene might now function similarly: within the realm of our media consumption, our desire to excise women's oppression manifests in pointing to the male gaze, to an image and the act of consuming it, rather than the materially ongoing machinations of patriarchy and how

53

to liberate women from it. What might it mean to stop running from sex, while resisting the impulse to simplify it or gloss over its enduring and troubling complexity?

In the era of ubiquitously accessible pornography, our sexuality is already being mediated consciously and subconsciously through our screens: the sex we watch shapes the sex we have. Is it not, therefore, even more important that we enlist the sex scene's powerfully moving imagery to break past the sexual scripts of patriarchy? Great sex scenes, those that are often complicated and ambivalent, that challenge us to think beyond the existing order, offer many paths to wade through the quagmire of sex: resourcing us to confront its ambiguities not searching for straw men or false liberation, but something closer to truth.

Our preoccupation with disavowing the male gaze has largely overshadowed the forward-looking possibilities for cinema contained in Mulvey's essay. A filmmaker herself, she was adamant that there was space for a radical, alternative mode of filmmaking that could challenge the patriarchal language, politics and aesthetics of mainstream cinema. It is to these films that we now turn: the wealth of brilliant and complicated depictions of sex that illuminate the gendered distribution of pleasure and power across the bedroom, the office, the fantasy. They are forever moving and politically important precisely because they suggest we will have to make and remake sex in flux.

Explicitly ruminating on the proximities between cinema and pornography, Bette Gordon's 1983 film *Variety* follows Christine, a woman who sells tickets at a porno theatre in '70s New York and becomes obsessed with a customer called Louie. She says it's just a job, but as she takes her smoke breaks inside the theatre, and we hear the overlapping soundtracks of women moaning and panting, it's clear that something within her has been unlocked. *Variety* is less concerned with condemning how the women being fucked on screen are mere erotic objects than it is in exploring the unblinking interest Christine has in being the one who watches; her presence at the box office means that at the threshold of sexual gratification, the anonymous spectator is momentarily thwarted by her looking right at him.

Variety thus positions Christine, not the men at the theatre, as voyeur. She begins to stalk Louie, which dovetails with her sexual awakening. Excluding the porn seen at the theatre, *Variety* does not contain a traditional sex scene – yet its most bracingly erotic sequence, a four-minute monologue Christine delivers while her boyfriend plays pinball, deserves to be considered one. Staring right at him, she tells a story about a man who spies on a naked woman in the throes of sexual ecstasy with a serpent, and then a tiger, before she seduces and fucks him too. While Christine narrates from his perspective and uses the objectifying language of male fantasy – the woman's body is "excitingly white", her "cunt wet and inviting", his cock "thrusting deeper, harder, over and over" – her boyfriend studiously avoids her eyes. This scene cuts us with the double-edged sword of women's erotic oppression: the violence of becoming a sexual object while one's own desire is invisibilised. Aligning herself with the male voyeur who gets what he wants, Christine displays the strange, ravenous force of her sexuality – which we take for granted in men – and humiliates her boyfriend's inability to acknowledge it. Can't a woman be turned on the way men are turned on? Can't she be the one with the hungry, desirous look? With this scene, Gordon – insistent on challenging "the existing culture from within" the bowels of patriarchy[70] – foregrounded the terrors and possibilities of adopting the male gaze in sex for oneself.

However, is there not sometimes pleasure in being the object of the voyeur's gaze? In Shinya Tsukamoto's 2002 film *A Snake Of June*, the perversity of the male voyeur is never denied: the director, in a self-flagellating move aimed not just at himself but at cinema too, casts himself as the film's Peeping Tom. Shot in a claustrophobic 4:3 aspect ratio and steeped in a blue tint that summons the cold artificiality of CCTV footage, *A Snake Of June* follows a call centre worker named Rinko (Asuka Kurosawa) who is mailed photographs of herself masturbating in her house. Subverting a traditional blackmail plot – albeit still with questionable methods – the voyeur's stated motive is to help Rinko liberate herself from the domestic repression of her sexless marriage. Having watched from afar, he has uncovered her exhibitionist desires and challenges her to follow his orders over the phone and "do what she wants" in public: wear a miniskirt without any underwear; walk through a shopping mall; buy herself a vibrator he can control remotely. Terrified, she obeys in exchange for his copy of the photographs, but after she successfully retrieves them and the man hangs up, her terror is shown to coexist with immense arousal. Returning to the public toilet cubicle where she was ordered to change her clothes earlier, she gives herself a shattering orgasm with her new vibrator.

A Snake Of June inverts the familiar power dynamic between male blackmailer and female victim so that Rinko's desires command the film – here, instead of punishing a woman for her sexuality, the voyeur sees her how she longs to be seen, and is recruited towards her ecstatic pleasure. Frequently cutting between heavy rain, water gushing out of pipes, and Rinko's moist face in the bath, the film's imagery drips with wetness: awash with the idea that a woman's erotic force could overpower the city's patriarchal infrastructure that attempts to contain it.

The coercion involved in Rinko reconnecting with her sexual agency only makes visible the impurity of negotiating life under patriarchy; perhaps there is never a clean break between oppression and the beginnings of what comes after. But what do we make of the fact that women enjoy looking at women as sexual objects – seeing herself as that object, like Rinko, or as the traditionally "male" spectator, like Christine – and that they enjoy looking at men that way, too? The female voyeur unsettles the solidity of the "male gaze" as an enemy to rally against, and complicates our male-centred understanding of visual pleasure. Frannie Avery, our protagonist played by Meg Ryan in Jane Campion's 2003 erotic thriller *In the Cut*, also begins as a voyeur. In one of its very first scenes, she descends into the basement of a bar – a spatial allegory for her subconscious desires – and sees a woman giving a police officer a blowjob, their faces shrouded in darkness. Stopped in her tracks, Frannie watches; the cop sees her, and pushes the woman's hair aside so Frannie can get a better view of his cock moving between her lips. When she goes home, a police detective named Malloy (Mark Ruffalo) is waiting in her stairwell to tell her that the body parts of a murdered woman have been found in her building. Angela Sands is the latest victim of a serial killer who gruesomely "disarticulates" women – a strangely clinical word that mesmerises Frannie coming out of Malloy's mouth – and whose signature flourish is leaving a wedding ring on his victims' fingers. That night, Frannie masturbates to the memory of the scene at the bar, imagining that it was Malloy she saw in that basement. We later find out that the woman giving the blowjob was Angela, right before she was murdered.

As Frannie is pulled deeper into the case, her attraction to Malloy intensifies alongside her suspicion that he may be the murderer. *In the Cut* – its title both a reference to the serial killer and slang for vagina – is perhaps the most stunning exploration of the entanglement between female desire and omnipresent patriarchal violence ever put to screen. Woozily, one shapeshifts into the other; fantasy and nightmare bleed into her reality. On her way home after a drink with Malloy, Frannie is mugged in a dark alley and left shaken. In her apartment, Malloy asks her to reenact what happened, role-playing as her assailant: "He must have come up from behind you. Was it his right arm, or his left?" he asks, cradling Frannie's neck in the crook of his arm. The memory of the attack is reimagined as an erotic, welcome touch: one that derives its charge precisely because of that echo of violence, and perhaps the possibility of it becoming violent once more. The camera lavishes attention on Frannie's nose tucked into the sleeve of Malloy's jacket, and on his thumb gradually drifting down to brush her nipple over the thin fabric of her dress. Then it lingers on her face. She turns back to look at him, and says, "All right."

We cut to Malloy in bed, placing his gun on the dresser, and Frannie bringing out a condom from the bathroom. Campion's film is cocooned in a soft-focus lens, which has the dual effect of making its violence more nauseating, and its intimate moments even more lush in sensation. Malloy begins to eat Frannie out from behind, and the blurry, gently handheld motions of the camera deny us a total-ising view of their bodies – rejecting pornography's almost sterile pursuit of maximising visibility, and instead aesthet-ically presenting a diffuse eroticism. Most important in this scene are Frannie's sounds, her hand reaching back to tangle in Malloy's hair; her foot protruding stiffly in pleasure and Malloy's move to kiss it; and of course, her face when she comes. A woman's pleasure, it turns out, is incredibly visible if you know where to look. But the scene's heady, erotic haze also translates Frannie's uncer-tainty about Malloy: that the man who knows how to give her body such indulgent pleasure might also be the one dismembering other women.

Much has been written about this groundbreaking depiction of Frannie consenting to sex – the moment where she gives Malloy the "all right" before going to bed – and the first time I watched *In the Cut*, I remember being stunned by this, too. Yet revisiting it over and over again, I believe what makes this scene so powerful is not so much the well-meaning idea, often bluntly phrased, that "consent is sexy": it's that Frannie thinks Malloy could be the killer, wants him and says yes to sex regardless, and the film does not blame her for it. If Frannie consented to sex with Malloy, and he really turned out to be the killer, would she deserve to be blamed for her death? Against the backdrop of patriarchal violence – the way it kills women both quickly with a knife and slowly with the humiliation or denial of their desire – does she enter into sex with Malloy on equal footing? In *Tomorrow Sex Will Be Good Again*, author Katherine Angel writes about how our attachment to consent as *the* "overarching framework for thinking about good and bad sex" means we "ignore a crucial aspect of being a person: that individuals do not bear equal relationships of power to one another."[71] The sex is not good just because Frannie agrees to it, as if this wipes away all its ambiguity and possibility for harm. It is good because, despite all the unspoken ways patriarchy conspires to punish, frustrate, or foreclose her access to pleasure, they both get there anyway.

"Now thinking back on the course of my passion, I was like one blind, unafraid of the dark," she whispers in one scene, reading a poem aloud. *In the Cut* is both deeply erotic and heavy with terror, mourning so many desiring women who paid with their lives for wanting sex, wanting marriage, wanting to be wanted. But it tells us that we deserve to survive the darkness, and that pleasure remains possible and necessary in spite of it: the only way out might be to feel our way through.

What is sex, after all, if not the bliss, pain, and beauty of how we are mutually undone? Part of the problem is how we forget all of us, not just women, are made vulnerable in sex. Steven Shainberg's 2002 film *Secretary* illustrates this – if at first unintuitively – with a lawyer and his secretary who begin a sadomasochistic relationship in his office. (Bonus points for the latent anticapitalism of these two not getting any work done because of all the spanking and petplay.) Foregrounding the power dynamic between male boss Mr. Grey and his female employee, Lee, the film's eventual claim feels even more subversive: that to be the one who submits is to be just as vulnerable and powerful as the one who dominates, because of how much one's pleasure cannot exist without the other. *Secretary* acknowledges our initial discomfort with eroticising the objectionable power difference between Grey and Lee, but coaxes us to look deeper. Through the heightened contrivance of sexual play between "boss" and "secretary", Grey and Lee's sadomasochistic relation in fact recognises what their hierarchical labour relation must disavow: the social construction of their roles, their interdependence, and the possibility of equality. As we watch Lee restrained with a spreader bar, crawling through the office on all fours, and Grey harnessing her into a saddle, what comes to the fore is the miracle of two people deciding to know each other so intimately. Dominance and submission are conceived of as a mutual give and take: cleaving away from the gendered dualisms of active/passive, masculine/feminine, powerful/powerless.

Eventually, Grey begins to withdraw from their relationship, panicked and ashamed, and Lee has to coax him back in: which is to say, be vulnerable and open to risk so he can be, too. When she stages a hunger strike in his office to convince him to return to her, a family friend brings her some 'feminist literature' to read: a wryly humourous gag that gestures to the opinion of many watching, surely, that Lee's desires are the result of internalised misogyny. Today, however, feminism has largely arrived at the consensus that we should listen to what a woman says about the sex she wants to have, no matter how much we might personally be incapable of understanding her. This is not just because we have a strong reason to believe what women tell us about their experiences, as philosopher Amia Srinivasan writes in *The Right to Sex*: "It is also, or perhaps primarily, an ethical claim: a feminism that trades too freely in notions of self-deception is a feminism that risks dominating the subjects it presumes to liberate."[72] Lee's final visitor is her father, who tells her, "Your soul and your body are your own, and yours to do with as you wish". She smiles. Our task as feminists might be one of holding contradiction, Srinivasan suggests. We must "treat as axiomatic our free sexual choices", while understanding that "such choices, under patriarchy, are rarely free."[73]

Secretary is, at its core, a pure-hearted exploration of sexuality as negotiation between partners; of the optimistic pursuit of desire giving one's life meaning; about a woman discovering what she wants, fighting for it, and convincing her shy, insecure dom to keep giving it to her. This remains true alongside our knowledge that our desires are still constituted under patriarchy – that they may not have taken this specific shape otherwise. Yet when Lee discovers she is aroused by being submissive, it is something that seems to emerge spontaneously within her, surprising her with its unexpected pleasure. As Angel beautifully puts it, desire is not something that lies within us, fully formed and ready for extraction: it "emerge[s] in interaction", meaning we sometimes don't know what we want, that we might find out what we want "only in the doing".[74] *Secretary* is a beguiling portrait of desire's eternally shifting nature, unable to be pinned down before the moment of its unruly, thrilling discovery.

Can we find ways to embrace and inhabit the perennial duality of pleasure and risk in sex under patriarchy – not just in spite of, but especially because of the strength of the scripts we are taught to limit ourselves with? Confronting that messiness, rife with contradiction and vulnerability, is where true ecstasy might await us. Asking us to look beyond the simplicity of the "male gaze", enlist it and remake it to our pleasure, and remain open to invention over and over again, these sex scenes might help us imagine how we get there. All of us, together, might begin to feel our way through the dark.

Chapter 4
The queer sex scene against representation

Art and culture is shaped by what we imagine to be possible, and what we imagine to be possible is shaped by art and culture. But today, when we talk about this feedback loop of possibility in relation to queer art, we seem unable to escape the discursive confines of "representation", which has become our primary tool for parsing media by or depicting anyone other than the cishet white man. Art for or by the marginalised is now largely evaluated through this lens: how good is this work at including previously excluded identities, and even better, in the mainstream?

'Representation' has become a conceptual cudgel, a statistic-motivated exercise that entails a strange, virtue-signalling logic. How many times has Pixar or Disney announced that so-and-so is the first gay character in the so-and-so franchise? The logic of representation has given us many cases like Officer Specter, the animated lesbian troll cop voiced by Lena Waithe in 2020's *Onward*, the Zootopia antelopes who were apparently the first ever gay couple in a Disney film, or the much-marketed first gay kiss in the *Star Wars* universe in *The Rise of Skywalker*. Between two unnamed extras, the kiss was less than a second long, and swiftly and easily cut when screened in countries where it would have threatened the studio's bottom line.

Unsurprisingly, an increase in "queer representation" has not meant more queer sex on screen. In exchange for inclusion in the mainstream, queer sexuality has been de-sexed so it can be put on sale. Queerness is to be tolerated if it is merely nominal, unchallenging to dominant and heteronormative structures; it is to be falsely, voraciously 'embraced' if there is money to be made in doing so. This is not to deny that seeing queerness on screen can be powerful and transformative, especially beyond these more cynical examples. But the regime of representation prescribes our relationship to art and reduces it to a stilted transaction: where all we need is to see ourselves in that queer person on screen, to flatten our multiplicity and bring our identities and desires into conformity with what has already been chosen for us. Instead of queerness being something we internally sense, something originating in our bodies about what we feel and what we want, we are coaxed into aligning ourselves with fixed and commodifiable ideas of queer identity.

Culture is an important field where homonormativity, theorised by the academic Lisa Duggan, is reproduced: the idea that good queers can be incorporated into the neoliberal nation-building project, which spans everything from access to the heteronormative good life (consumerism, monogamous marriage, home-ownership, raising children) to demanding that queers have the right to serve in the military. The homonormative regime of media representation, where inclusion or belonging in the dominant structure is the end goal and the limit of our imagination, goes hand-in-hand with a queer political programme which accepts the terms and options made available by our oppressors. Today, popular queer politics has become about appealing to the government to distribute our rights, our healthcare, our seat at the (bloodstained) table as queers: surrendering to the nation-state as gatekeeper of the lives we do or do not deserve to live. Queer identity has also been enlisted to justify wars; to position the 'liberated' and 'free' West as superior to the sexually 'backward' Middle East; to close liberal ranks around genocidal politicians, who must stay in power because queer people at home are more important than queer people being bombed by our governments.

If this is queerness, I don't want it. I am instead drawn to queer theorist José Esteban Muñoz's declaration that "queerness is not yet here", that it is what tells us "this world is not enough".[75] This recalls Audre Lorde's writing on the power of the erotic, which she understood as "a grave responsibility, projected from within each of us, not to settle for the convenient, the shoddy, the conventionally expected, nor the merely safe."[76] The queer erotic connects this internal feeling to an expansive, outward-reaching desire to bring forward new worlds for ourselves and those we are in relation with. To Muñoz, queerness is the knowledge that the past is a realm of possibility, available to us in the present to aid the dawn of a new futurity: a folding so that all three corners touch.[77] The queer sex scene is an aesthetic artefact that enacts this very touching. The sprawling timeline of the films discussed herein is evidence itself against the teleological narrative of LGBT pragmatism's rights-based progress. Sometimes there is more futurity to be found in glancing backwards to seventy years ago, which may – in the sex scene's ability to bring us closer in time and space to queer sensations, subjects, and desires – equip us to transcend the standstill of the present.

These queer sex scenes are examples of what anthropologist Gayle Rubin calls "scary sex": to fuck in a way that crosses the line between "sexual order and chaos", invoking the establishment's fear that "something unspeakable will skitter across."[78] Yes, these are orgies, public sex, sex with the 'wrong bodies', sex full of 'sin', sex across political lines – but just as importantly, they are creative texts about how to fuck against the state together, about evading surveillance, capture, and assimilation. Muñoz describes how certain queer art allows us to understand our "desire for politics alongside the politics of desire".[79] The unspeakable thing that skitters across may be no less than a reclamation of our collective power.

A silent film made in 1950, *Un chant d'amour* is novelist, playwright, and activist Jean Genet's only film. It is set in a French prison, where we watch the indefatigable creativity of queer desire overcome the carceral violence of the state that wishes to thwart it. *Un chant d'amour* begins with a bouquet of flowers being swung from one hand, stuck through and outside the prison bars, towards another hand trying to grasp it. Through the prison warden's voyeuristic eye, we peer into each cell to see the inmates masturbating, relishing in their own bodies. Most centrally, we are privy to the erotic connection between an older man and the younger man in the cell adjoining his. The former passionately kisses the wall between them, grinds his body against it. He lights a cigarette: then, pushing a hollow piece of straw into the tiniest hole in the wall, blows the smoke into the adjoining cell and his lover's mouth. It is a stunningly erotic gesture, one that finds within the carceral and colonial architecture of the prison an apparatus of sexual opportunity, the glory hole.

Queerness is what allows such possibility to be sensed; it is the inventive way we make our bodies extend through hostile space towards the other. If the prison is a mass of bodies kept apart, such togetherness is a threatening force: so when the warden angrily enters the older man's cell, it is his gun, the state's phallus, that he forces into the prisoner's mouth. While being brutalised by the warden, the older man escapes reality by fantasising about running through the countryside with his lover. It is a magically apt example of Muñoz's articulation of queerness as a "mode of desiring" that allows us to envision a world outside the "prison house" of the here and now.[80] At the end of the film, when the warden's back is turned, we see the bouquet of flowers – its promise of tenderness, intimacy, survival in the midst of abjection – finally being grasped. 75 years later, *Un chant d'amour* still feels incredibly futuristic in its imagination of queer sexual pleasure that outmanoeuvres state surveillance and punishment. Banned and censored internationally for decades due to its explicit homosexual content, its survival is another act of escape and resilience; Genet himself was in and out of prison for crimes including homosexual acts.

I find echoes of *Un chant d'amour* in the 2019 Georgian film *And Then We Danced*, about a young dancer in the ultra-masculine National Georgian Ensemble named Merab who falls in love with another dancer, Irakli. Cast and crew received death threats while shooting,[81] masked individuals reportedly tried to break into the cinema with pyrotechnics during the film's Georgian premiere,[82] and nationalist and religious groups attempted to cancel the screening in protest against the "sin of sodomy".[83] Sodomy has been historically, infamously named 'the crime against nature'. How beautiful, then, that *And Then We Danced*'s sex scenes extend the pastoral line of possibility seen in Genet's film by taking place outdoors. For Merab and Irakli, this is out of necessity so they will not be discovered by others, but the way they have sex in the dirt, outside the suffocating house of patriarchal tradition, affirms their queerness as part of Georgia's natural landscape. Both the film's sex scenes take place in front of the same boulder outside a family friend's home, its contours just large enough to obscure the two men's bodies from view. Nature is re-signified as a place of queer refuge, camouflage, and possibility; the boulder becomes a monument marking a desire path, the line created by those who venture off the path they are supposed to follow.

Touching this boulder, touching these films, I recall scholar Sara Ahmed's writing on desire lines and the oft-forgotten "orientation" of sexual orientation: that sexuality is a matter of who we turn to face, who we are close to, of "how we inhabit spaces as well as "who" or "what" we inhabit spaces with."[84] Ahmed writes about how, by virtue of our membership in the nation or other constructed communities, we are placed on a path of the "good life" that politically requires us to face a certain direction: to "turn some ways and not others".[85] Queerness redirects our attention towards those who are not immediately in the circumscribed field of the touchable, those we may have to turn around to reach. I emphasise the "sexual" of sexual orientation too, not wanting to lose sight of how it is the erotic that sets this in motion, the desiring body that makes this turn possible. Desire is unruly and – excitingly – liable to lead us astray.

In Cheryl Dunye's 1996 film *The Watermelon Woman*, the first feature film ever directed by an 'out' Black lesbian, Dunye plays Cheryl, a filmmaker working on a documentary about the life of a forgotten Black actress, who she eventually discovers was a lesbian in a relationship with a white female director. Dealing with questions of erased Black history and the relationship between self and subject in her film, Cheryl is pulled in by her attraction to Diana, a well-to-do white girl she meets at work. Her circle of Black lesbian friends disapprove, and Cheryl herself admits she is shocked by "the whole sleeping with Diana thing"; something that connects Cheryl and her documentary subject is how to navigate one's desire as a Black lesbian, especially when that desire seems to cause friction with one's politics. Yet the sex scene between Cheryl and Diana, named "the hottest dyke sex scene ever recorded on celluloid" by the Philadelphia City Paper, is a revelation. A luxuriously tactile montage of bare skin – feet slowly dragged up calves, hands tracing the contours of a back, lips closing over nipples, spit gleaming on chests – the scene is a reminder that quite physically, we come to know ourselves and the bounds of our body through touch, and that through touch, we might momentarily be allowed to enjoy our skin as distinct from its meanings: as just skin. *The Watermelon Woman* is miles too clever to do anything as inelegant as reach for the post-racial, but nevertheless, its eroticism seems to emerge from the political dilemma of the present and sense an open, pleasure-oriented future.

Touch is also an overpowering force in Park Chanwook's 2016 film *The Handmaiden*. A labyrinthine tale set in Japanese-occupied Korea, it follows a Korean thief named Sook-hee who agrees to work together with a conman to rob a rich Japanese heiress, Lady Hideko, of her fortune: Sook-hee will pretend to be a handmaiden, get close to the heiress, and convince her to marry him. Unbeknownst to Sook-hee, Lady Hideko is also collaborating with the conman, and is the true mastermind behind the operation. Desiring her escape from her abusive uncle's mansion – where she is forced to read pornography to him and other members of the colonial elite – Hideko intends to put Sook-hee away in an asylum under her own name, swapping their identities. Yet brought together in the close proximity of Hideko's chambers, the women find themselves sexually attracted to each other, complicating their mutual plans of betrayal. In a scene where Sook-hee is helping Hideko undress, the camera lingers on the fetishised, feminine haptics of silk gloves on bare skin and fingers unlacing corsets. Desire affectively overwhelms the classed, ethnicised, and colonial hierarchy between the two women; it is posited as a force powerful enough to cross 'enemy lines'. Hideko and Sook-hee's romantic and sexual union eventually means they will demand a different outcome to their story – deciding to abandon their respective schemes so they can free each other, together. Desire can surprise us, suddenly revealing a path we never knew was there.

The sex scenes between Hideko and Sook-hee possess a meticulously crafted imagery. When they engage in the "infamously pornographic act of scissoring", as academic Jasmine Hu describes it, what is radically presented is the opportunity for sameness, for "two whole bodies" giving and receiving abundant pleasure through lesbian sex across colonial lines.[86] The hyper-stylised aesthetic symmetry of these scenes calls attention to how the two women's bodies, through sex, shed their attachments to the hierarchical separation of oppressor/victim, coloniser/colonised, manipulator/manipulated – to the contrary, Hideko and

Sook-hee almost appear to meld together. Given the film's identity theft plot, this loss of self is both threatening and ripe with possibility. Sex becomes their first act of collaboration, paving the way for them to devise a queer escape from colonial violence. The film ends with them having sex once more as they chart their getaway on a boat bound for Shanghai. There is an important ambivalence to this scene: using silver bells as sex toys, a direct echo of one of the pornographic stories Hideko was forced to read to her uncle's audience, Hideko and Sook-hee experiment with resignifying the objects of oppression for their pleasure. Whether they will find a way to transcend it is an open question left by the film's ending, which never grants us the closure of seeing them arrive at any fixed destination, geographically or otherwise. Leaving us with the image of their ship sailing dreamily into the night sky, their vocalisations of sexual bliss slowly fading into the distance, *The Handmaiden*'s ending overtly summons Muñoz's vision of queerness as always oriented towards the horizon, an "insistence on potentiality ... for another world".[87] One imagines that Hideko and Sook-hee will continue exploring avenues for survival, avenues for pleasure, beyond what the film's narrative permits us to witness. This echoes how the sociologist and writer Angela Jones understands queerness as an ongoing process of becoming, one that demands repeated "experimentations with alterity".[88] We may not arrive at queerness, but it might be what allows us to turn again and again towards those we are supposed to disavow, in defiance of the predetermined trajectories our bodies are supposed to inherit.

The assimilationist rhetoric of representation thus threatens to foreclose the unlimited potential of queerness' glimmering waters, its refusal to let any reflection settle into a fixed image. I'm always thinking about what my friend Rho said to me: "I'm not looking for a mirror in my media. I'm looking for possibility, for trans invention. I don't want to be sold something I already have." The cinematic language of Isabel Sandoval's 2019 film *Lingua Franca* – and particularly that of its sex scenes – strikes me as such an example. *Lingua Franca* stars writer-director Sandoval as Olivia, an undocumented Filipina immigrant and trans woman who works as a carer for the elderly Olga in Brooklyn, and who develops an attraction to Olga's grandson, Alex. One day, when Alex offers to take Olivia to the post office, they happen across an immigration raid; Alex drags a terrified Olivia back to the car, where she explains she has been paying a man to fake a relationship with her so she can marry him for a green card. When they get home, Olivia passionately pulls Alex in for a kiss. It is an impulse to claim sexual and bodily autonomy in spite of the ways she has just been reminded that the state surveils bodies like hers, categorises them by nationality and sex, deems some bodies illegal and others not.

In the sex scene that follows, subjectivity does not lie with Alex. Our anticipation of the stereotypical, traumatic moment of him 'finding out' she is trans – rendering her an object and re-enacting the state's xenophobic narrative that she should be punished for what she 'hides' – is foiled, to our relief. Instead, the scene's subjectivity lies with extended shots of Olivia's face, contorting in pleasure. "There's a certain fixation and obsession with trans bodies, so the sex scene is the opposite of that," Sandoval says in an interview with Autostraddle. "She's feeling this creeping anxiety about the dangers she might be exposing herself to by being sexually intimate with a man who isn't aware she's trans. But it's important to show those two things together ... her trepidation and fear ... coupled with her enjoyment and sexual pleasure."[89] Sex is posited as a place where subjecthood comes into being: deciding to enter into risk as well as pleasure is an affirmation of Olivia's autonomy. Recuperating the cerebral as intertwined with the bodily, *Lingua Franca*'s sex scene – by what it demands us to look at and what it resolutely refuses to show – rejects mainstream cinema's transphobic impulse to fetishise a 'reveal'. This sex scene is explicitly pitched against state surveillance and violence, carving out space for trans dignity and subjectivity.

Is sex not somewhere we come to understand ourselves more deeply through contact with others? Perhaps it has never been more of an identity quest than in John Cameron Mitchell's 2006 film *Shortbus*, where characters across New York converge weekly at its titular sexual and artistic salon, inspired by the city's queer underground scene of the early 2000s.[90] The film follows an ensemble of characters: primarily Sofia, a sex therapist who has never had an orgasm; James, a gay man secretly filming his suicide note; and Severin, an alienated dominatrix. In its opening scene, we swoop through an animated diorama of New York to see Sofia having acrobatic sex with her husband, James sadly filming his penis pissing in the bathwater before self-fellating and ejaculating on his own face, and Severin whipping a talkative client in a hotel room overlooking Ground Zero. They are simultaneous but apart; their paths will intertwine at Shortbus. When the orgasm-questing Sofia arrives there, she looks hesitantly at the orgy room, where a writhing mass of bodies are getting it on in many different configurations. The club's mistress, Justin Vivian Bond, asks her how the big O is coming along; she responds that she must have some sort of "neural clog" between her brain and her clitoris. This prompts Justin to unveil the film's arrestingly optimistic thesis:

> Don't think of it as a clog. Think of it as some sort of magical circuit board – a motherboard filled with desire that travels all over the world, that touches

you, that touches me, that connects everybody. You just have to find the right circuitry. Look at all these people out there: they're just trying to find the right connection.

This is a utopian vision of interdependence: a move from individualism to the electric possibilities sparked by the collective. Shortbus is where Severin develops a friendship with Sofia, giving her the authentic human connection she craves; where James crosses paths with the voyeur who will save his life; where Sofia confronts issues with her marriage and sexuality by trying on different queer connections, even though she initially says she "isn't wired that way". Sex becomes a metaphor for how we transform each others' lives through contact, vulnerability, and intimacy; sex is the social itself. Yet it is never relegated to mere symbolism in *Shortbus*, which contains many explicit, unsimulated sex acts – including a three-way where the US national anthem is enthusiastically belted into a man's asshole mid-rimjob. Very much an American film (it's *so* patriotic, but gets away with it for being so irresistibly warm), *Shortbus* is a window into a post-9/11 queer optimism about the redemptive power of togetherness and plurality, exemplified by the orgy room being named the 'Sex Not Bombs' room. Set against the real-life New York blackout of 2003, the film depicts this city-wide event as coinciding with (or caused by) Sofia's despairing failure to masturbate to orgasm. Everyone gathers at a candlelit Shortbus, their various arcs on the way to some form of resolution; there is kissing, reconciliation, heavy petting, singing. Sofia is approached by the beautiful couple she locked eyes with in the orgy room, and they begin to kiss and touch her. As a marching band arrives and the singing escalates to a triumphant, celebratory chorus, Sofia finally orgasms for the first time. We zoom back out to the diorama of New York – lights are coming back on, all across the city. If orgasm is a momentary annihilation of the self, and if sex is, as theorists Lauren Berlant and Lee Edelman write, a threat to our "putative sovereignty" as individuals,[91] *Shortbus* asks us to see this as a revelatory moment brimming with hope, one that reminds us of our profoundly interconnected existence.

I came across another depiction of group sex as a matter of electricity in Fujisawa Isao's 1974 film, *Bye Bye Love*. Our two protagonists – the nihilistic Utamaro and the elegant, genderfluid Giko – have decided to hire a sex worker, partially due to Giko's perceived lack of sexual experience. When the sex worker arrives, Utamaro says, "Do that one in the bed first," gesturing to Giko. When Utamaro uses a masculine pronoun for Giko, it only prompts a humorously offhand, "So you guys are queers? Weird…" from the sex worker as she strips off. As she begins her machinations on Giko's naked chest, the latter says to Utamaro, "I'm not feeling anything." Absent-mindedly fiddling with a lamp, Utamaro sticks his finger in the socket and is given an electric shock, spawning an idea. Disemboweling the hotel room's radio to reveal its innards of cable, he wraps all three of them with live wires up and down their bodies and in their mouths; whenever they kiss, all three are jolted apart with the shock before collapsing back together. Even more literally than in *Shortbus*, sex is about finding the right circuitry. As the camera grazes over a chaotic tangle of feet, legs, and wires, we see a vision of sex without tops and bottoms, where both gender and the penetrator/penetrated binary melts away in favour of polymorphous sensation, where any contact point between one's skin and the other's becomes an erogenous zone. Fifty years ago, *Bye Bye Love* gave us a glimpse of trans technologies of pleasure: which is never so much about the cutting-edge as it is about actualising the latent queerness of the everyday, about the futuristic impulse it takes to sense a radio as not just a radio, but so much more.

It is an artefact of queer science-fiction-sex, which brings us to the scene I offer as a climax: the orgy in season one, episode six of the Wachowskis' television series, *Sense8*. Like *Shortbus*, *Sense8* is an ensemble narrative that comes alive at its characters' points of convergence. Its central science-fiction conceit is that these conver-gences happen in an alternate, overlapping dimension of perception: each of the narrative's eight "sensates" are able to simultaneously "visit" each others' realities through a shared psychic link. The show's towering, transnational ambition spans South Korea, India, Germany, Kenya, Iceland, Spain, and the US, collapsing the earthly distance between them. As the sensates habituate themselves to the bodily and perceptual experience of feeling what each other feels, it is no surprise that what eventually opens up is a multidimensional sexual possibility.

The scene in question is precipitated by Nomi, whose girlfriend has rescued her from the hospital where she was to be lobotomised: a procedure meant to sever her link to the other sensates. Nomi begins to kiss her, feeling vitalised and aroused. "It might be the fact that I still have my brain, it might be the fact that you saved my life …" As is *Sense8*'s innovative style, this scene is first intertwined with several others happening contemporaneously – Will at the gym; Lito and his boyfriend lifting weights on their balcony; Wolfgang reclining naked in a public bath – before they begin to merge. The scene expands by folding in on itself: we see Nomi kissing Lito's boyfriend and Lito kissing Nomi's girlfriend; Nomi and Lito touching Wolfgang in the bath; Lito tangling his hand in Will's tank top as he drips with sweat from doing crunches, pulling him close to Nomi's mouth. We gradually witness all of them orgiastically having sex in each place, at the same time. Their bodies move together in slow-motion, which has the effect of making every second seem impossibly decadent and heavy with sensation: a greater density of feeling than a singular, individual present could ever hold.

Sense8 is perhaps the most accomplished moving image depiction of what Muñoz calls "ecstatic time": moments of queer ecstasy and pleasure that eject us from the linearity of straight time and its political disappointments.[92] What this scene presents, against the violently atomising discourses of individualism or the nation, is the dizzying potential for multiple and many solidarities all at once: of alliances and shared encounters across bodies and borders, broadening who it is we respond to and who we are *responsible* for politically. *Sense8* ambitiously extends a trans and queer posture of thinking and feeling across other(ed) bodies to thinking and feeling across races, genders, ethnicities, and nationalities: something the show positions as an evolutionary advantage, allowing the sensates to draw on each other's strengths to overcome their adversaries. But it is this sex scene that most viscerally translates *Sense8*'s utopian conceit into something we are asked to feel with our bodies: a boundless and all-encompassing empathy where those far away are brought near, where our pain, pleasure, and survival is physically experienced as collective beyond those we are in immediate community with. Here, queer desire literally extends to touch others who "might not have otherwise been reachable within the body horizon of the social."[93] The ecstatic orgy that freely entangles trans, lesbian, gay, and straight bodies together is a vision of what the author ME O'Brien calls "erotic solidarity", distinct from the essentialist politics of (gay or lesbian) identity in its far-reaching desire for livable futures for all.[94]

Showrunner Lana Wachowski describes her narratives as an "assault" on the dominant cultural notion that everything is static.[95] What is destabilised by *Sense8*'s lush sensory assault is the notion that our political responsibilities should congeal along identitarian lines, be that of gender, sexuality, or the nation. Imagine the threat we would pose to the forces that oppress and divide us if we could truly sense other bodies as our own – even those we are told are too different, too distant, too undeserving of our attention. Is it any wonder why mainstream 'representation' quietly works to defang queer eroticism, in fear of what boundaries and borders might be shattered; what power we might find in feeling and acting as a mass of interconnected bodies? These sex scenes map far-reaching networks of interdependence: disobedient intimacies that evade institutional capture and recognition to become ungovernable. They might be a portal through which we are called to act again and again on our utopian desires, so that somewhere on the horizon of possibility, we might – in the most erotically and politically robust sense of the phrase – finally come together.

Conclusion

My hands are cold, it is winter again, and as I write this at the tail end of 2024, we have been waking up every single day to abject and unfathomable horror on our screens, each day somehow more unimaginably cruel than the last, for more than a year. Thinking about the passage of time is incredibly disorienting. It has been a painful and absurd time to be writing a book, or to be doing anything else at all.

I know this is a book about sex scenes. That's what I've said to most people who have asked about it, partially because I like the prurience of leaving it there. But it's mostly because I think the task of unravelling how my feelings about sex and its representations are entangled with everything I grieve, despair over, and dare to hope for politically will remain a lifelong project – one I've aspired to embark on here. Perhaps it seems scandalous, at a moment so lacerated with crisis everywhere we look, to be spending so much time thinking about sex. But as anthropologist Gayle Rubin observes, it is precisely "when we live with the possibility of unthinkable destruction"[96] that sexuality becomes mobilised as a political minefield: a highly charged symbolic battleground littered with scarecrows and moral panics invariably deployed to discipline us into obedience, to raze over those of us who do not wish to "quietly and politely make house in this killing machine", in the words of artist and AIDS activist David Wojnarowicz.

Tracing the gradual disappearance of sex and eroticism from our screen culture, *Revolutionary Desires* argues that this is politically salient: if the relationship we cultivate with our media is disengaged, disembodied, and passive, it makes sense that what we see on the news no longer moves us. If we can be shamed away from sex and innate sources of pleasure, consumer capitalism easily annexes our wants and desires. If the panic around sex can be, once again, enlisted to bolster hegemonic forms of privatisation like the nuclear family, we turn inwards again and again, shutting our doors on a world where our survival is intertwined regardless.

When I think about the outcry over the sex scene, I think about how 'protecting the children' never means taking them out of poverty. I think about how 'keeping them safe' never means ensuring they can live their adult years on a planet not ravaged by climate disaster. I think about how many young people in this country have just lost access to safe, necessary, and long-established healthcare like puberty blockers that would have made life so much more liveable for them. I think about how we have decided some children deserve to live and others do not. I think about how many times I've seen a queer person say "genocide is bad" and the response is "they would throw you off a roof in Gaza". I think about how the settler colonial occupying force known as the IDF, which raises the rainbow flag and is considered one of the most progressive and LGBT-friendly militaries in the world, shoots children point-blank, opens fire on starving people in line for bread, and gleefully takes photos of themselves raiding and wearing Palestinian women's underwear. I think about how in the vast majority of countries where homosexuality is a crime, this is because of a penal code instituted by British imperialism. I think about those currently in prison here, some of them queer and some of them as young as 21 years old, who are facing inhumane and repressive terrorism charges for interrupting the flow of UK weapons supplying a genocide.

But I also think about how something as simple as a condom filled with flammable liquids is enough to send settlers running, exposing the cowardice and fragility of the occupying regime.[97] About babies being born in Gaza and fiercely loved, their survival fought for as the survival of the land, in spite of. I think about the queer map of

Palestine[98] dotted with stories, every single one an entire universe of memory and desire and grief that refuses to disappear under rubble, this impulse to say *yes* we are here and we live on, in spite of. I think about friends and neighbours and perfect strangers and lovers – all of these desiring, refusing bodies all over the world – holding the line, in spite of.

Sex is not going to be the revolution, and neither is cinema. But I do believe they are some of the many portals in our everyday lives to feelings of revolutionary impulse, no matter how nascent: the same way fucked-up things like anti-homeless architecture or seeing your friends forced to crowdfund for essential healthcare can stir something in our gut, so might encounters with art that deliver us glimpses of a different world, or experiences that reconnect us to our bodies and those of others. From *The Matrix Reloaded*'s rave to *Shortbus*' circuitboard of connection, we have seen how the desiring pull that binds us together in sex is perhaps one and the same with that which links our arms together on a picket line, using our collective weight and presence as a mass of dissenting people – it is a sensory and political ecstasy that explodes the atomised boundaries of the individual. Our investment in the erotic should be an open-ended call to feel it in the act of cooking for our friends and lovers, in allowing a beautiful and challenging piece of art to move us, in the day-to-day admin of organising work, in sensing the collective as an extension of our own bodies: but most of all, to act on that feeling in our bones that the world as it is cannot be enough for us. This is radically opposed to an escapist hedonism; it is rooted in the day-by-day transformation of the quotidian and the material.

Something as seemingly trivial or leisurely as the cinema available to us, and the cinema we seek out, is thus deeply linked with our political psyches and idea-tional resources – with reproducing the border between what we have and what we are coaxed into believing is possible. A homogenous and 'risk'-averse screen culture, in which producers and consumers alike disavow sex as either pointless or immoral, is one part of a cultural apparatus designed to keep us believing that the ease of unchallenging, disembodied consumerism, instead of real and complex human connection, is the way to cope with a broken-down present. For how much the sex scene has been demonised, I am regularly stunned by how it is often no more and no less than an extension of the mundane narrative of life: which is to say, that extraordinary, beautiful, confusing, heartbreaking, and momentarily transformative things extend out of the everyday all the time, because the everyday is all there is.

Audre Lorde's words on self-care being an act of resistance, adrienne maree brown's writing on pleasure activism, and other care and pleasure-oriented approaches to politics have inevitably been ripe for commod-ification: for the de-contextualised social media graphic or tasteful slogan aimed to soothe our guilt under the guise of radical action. But this is far from cause to abandon pleasure. It is instead proof – as the proponents of critical hedonism suggest – that pleasure has been made scarce precisely so we continue desiring things that keep us congenial to global capitalism. Yet we can relearn and rediscover pleasure in what enables us to build a more collective, collaborative, and just reality. Collectively transforming what we desire – and how – means refusing the violent and abject choices we currently call "politics" in the world as it is. Desire must be urgently enlisted to bring forward the horizon of a liberating futurity, to create the conditions under which the world as we know it gives way to something new.

The sex scene is not a script – although there can be something incredibly erotic about acting out a bodily memory of something we watch on screen – but as Linda Williams writes in her seminal work *Screening Sex*, "We do not simply imitate what we see, we play with it too."[99] What might spill forth, warm and lush and desiring, if we dared to play with the revolutionary impulses it might spark in us? The sex scenes in this book critique capitalism and find the energy to break past it; they experiment with risking and reinventing pleasure under patriarchy; most crucially, they refuse to surrender to the violence of the present, and they refuse to leave anyone behind. Feel it: that outward-reaching ecstasy, the way it senses so much more possibility than the here and now. Follow it into the future.

References

1   "'Challengers' Review: Luca Guadagnino and Zendaya Serve Up a Smart and Sexy Tennis Drama About Three Players in Search of the Perfect Match" David Ehrlich, *IndieWire*, 12 April 2024. indiewire.com/criticism/movies/challengers-movie-review-zendaya-1234973713/. Accessed 31 July 2024.

2   "have the "anti sex scene" people graduated to being against the empirical fact of sexuality? these are straightforward descriptions of the framing in one scene, and how eroticism is expressed through the weather in another. they're acting like I shouldn't be allowed near schools." @davidehrlich. *Twitter*, 12 April 2024, 11:15PM, twitter.com/davidehrlich/status/1778909828678820243. Accessed 31 July 2024.

3   "CSS Teens & Screens 2023: Romance or Nomance?" Rivas-Lara, S., Kotecha, H., Pham, B., & Uhls, Y.T., *Center for Scholars & Storytellers*, October 2023. scholarsandstorytellers.com/css-teens-and-screens-2023. Accessed 31 July 2024.

4   "New stats show that there's less sex than ever before in films" Emma Guinness, *The Independent*, 3 May 2024. independent.co.uk/arts-entertainment/films/news/film-sex-scenes-less-nudity-statistics-b2539035.html. Accessed 31 July 2024.

5   Linda Williams, *Screening Sex*. Duke University Press, 2008. p.29-30

6   Ibid. p.10

7   Ibid. p.1-2

8   "Gael García Bernal's Closet Picks" *CRITERION*, 3 January 2024. youtube.com/watch?v=oJxXni9bo3g&ab_channel=criterioncollection. Accessed 16 January 2025.

9   "Everyone is Beautiful and No One is Horny" Raquel S. Benedict, *Blood Knife,* 14 February 2021. bloodknife.com/everyone-beautiful-no-one-horny/. Accessed 16 January 2025.

10   "Eternals' awful sex scene is kind of clever the second time around" Charles Pulliam-Moore, *The Verge*, 13 January 2022. theverge.com/22880740/eternals-sex-scene-disney-plus. Accessed 16 January 2025.

11   "Kumail Nanjiani's 'Eternals' Workout" Charles Thorp, *Men's Journal*, 26 November 2021. mensjournal.com/health-fitness/kumail-nanjianis-workout. Accessed 16 January 2025.

12   Ibid.

13   Ibid.

14   "Review: Marvel's "The Eternals" is oppressively beautiful, puzzlingly bad" John Wenzel, *The Denver Post*, 9 November 2021. denverpost.com/2021/11/08/review-marvel-the-eternals/. Accessed 16 January 2025.

15   "'Eternals': The ponderous jibber-jabber and pointless battles seem like they'll never end" Richard Roeper, *Chicago Sun Times*, 2 November 2021. chicago.suntimes.com/movies-and-tv/2021/11/2/22755839/eternals-review-marvel-movie-chloe-zhao-richard-madden-gemma-chan-kumail-nanjiani. Accessed 16 January 2025.

16   "Kumail Nanjiani says he needed therapy after bad reviews for Marvel's Eternals" Annabel Rackham, *BBC News*, 8 February 2024. bbc.co.uk/news/entertainment-arts-68238261. Accessed 16 January 2025.

17   "Everyone is Beautiful and No One is Horny" Raquel S. Benedict, *Blood Knife,* 14 February 2021. bloodknife.com/everyone-beautiful-no-one-horny/. Accessed 16 January 2025.

18   "First date but she only speaks brainrot" @bryce_cohen, *Instagram*, 6 May 2024, instagram.com/p/C6oYCwtLUJP/. Accessed 16 Jan 2025

19   Erich Fromm, *To Have or to Be?* Continuum, 2008. p.120-121

20   "Everyone is Beautiful and No One is Horny" Raquel S. Benedict, *Blood Knife,* 14 February 2021. bloodknife.com/everyone-beautiful-no-one-horny/. Accessed 16 January 2025.

21   "The Puritanical Eye: Hyper-mediation, Sex on Film, and the Disavowal of Desire" Carlee Gomes, *Specchio Scuro*, 25

November 2023. specchioscuro.it/the-puritanical-eye-hyper-mediation-sex-on-film-and-the-disavowal-of-desire/. Accessed 16 January 2025.

22   "Matt Damon Sweats From His Scalp While Eating Spicy Wings | Hot Ones" *First We Feast*, 5 August 2021. youtube.com/watch?v=yaXma6K9mzo&ab_channel=FirstWeFeast. Accessed 16 January 2025.

23   Linda Williams, *Screening Sex*. Duke University Press, 2008. p.19

24   "The Puritanical Eye: Hyper-mediation, Sex on Film, and the Disavowal of Desire" Carlee Gomes, *Specchio Scuro*, 25 November 2023. specchioscuro.it/the-puritanical-eye-hyper-mediation-sex-on-film-and-the-disavowal-of-desire/. Accessed 16 January 2025.

25   "'You' Star Penn Badgley Wanted No More Intimacy Scenes On His Netflix Show, So The Creator Said Fine" Lynette Rice, *Deadline*, 9 February 2023. deadline.com/2023/02/you-star-penn-badgley-season-four-no-intimacy-scenes-netflix-1235254824/. Accessed 16 January 2025.

26   "Kids want one thing and it's the return of the Hays Code" @GuyLodge. *Twitter*, 12 February 2023, 3:39AM, twitter.com/GuyLodge/status/1624614197047750656. Accessed 16 January 2025.

27   "Neal McDonough Admits Putting God And His Family First Has Been 'Hard' On His Career (Exclusive)" *Closer Weekly*, 5 January 2019. closerweekly.com/posts/neal-mcdonough-admits-putting-god-and-his-family-first-was-hard-on-his-career-exclusive/. Accessed 16 January 2025.

28   Linda Williams, *Screening Sex*. Duke University Press, 2008. p.181.

29   "The Puritanical Eye: Hyper-mediation, Sex on Film, and the Disavowal of Desire" Carlee Gomes, *Specchio Scuro*, 25 November 2023. specchioscuro.it/the-puritanical-eye-hyper-mediation-sex-on-film-and-the-disavowal-of-desire/. Accessed 16 January 2025.

30   adrienne maree brown, *Pleasure Activism*. AK Press, 2019. p.6-7

31   "Uses of the Erotic: The Erotic as Power" From *Sister Outsider* by Audre Lorde. Crossing Press, 1987.

32   Linda Williams, *Screening Sex*. Duke University Press, 2008. p.13

33   Mark Fisher, *Capitalist Realism*. Zer0 Books, 2009. p.2

34   David Graeber, *The Utopia of Rules: On Technology, Stupidity, and the Secret Joys of Bureaucracy*. Melville House, 2015. p.89

35   Ibid.

36   Mihaela Mihai, *Political Memory and the Aesthetics of Care: The Art of Complicity and Resistance*. Stanford University Press, 2022. p.37

37   Linda Williams, *Screening Sex*. Duke University Press, 2008. p.18

38   Mark Fisher, *Capitalist Realism*. Zer0 Books, 2009. p.16

39   Kristen R. Ghodsee. *Why Women Have Better Sex Under Socialism*. Vintage Books, 2018. p.110

40   Ibid. p.135

41   Ibid. p.115

42   Chris Rodley. *Cronenberg on Cronenberg*. Faber, 1996. p.199

43   "'Crash' finds way round censor" David Lister, *The Independent*, 2 June 1997. independent.co.uk/news/crash-finds-way-round-censor-1253905.html. Accessed 16 January 2025.

44   Chris Rodley. *Cronenberg on Cronenberg*. Faber, 1996, p.199

45   Brottman, M., & Sharrett, C. (2002). The End of the Road: David Cronenberg's "Crash" and the Fading of the West. Literature/Film Quarterly, 30(2), 126-132. jstor.org/stable/43797082

46   Ibid.

47   Fukuyama, F. (1989). The End of History? The National Interest, 16, 3-18. https://www.jstor.org/stable/24027184

48   Brottman, M., & Sharrett, C. (2002). The End of the Road: David Cronenberg's "Crash" and the Fading of the West. Literature/Film Quarterly, 30(2), 126-132. jstor.org/stable/43797082

49   Chris Rodley. *Cronenberg on Cronenberg*. Faber, 1996. p.189

50   Jacques Derrida, *Specters of Marx: The State of the Debt, the Work of Mourning and the New International*. Routledge, 1994. p.106.

51   Mark Fisher, *Capitalist Realism*. Zer0 Books, 2009. p.15

52   Brottman, M., & Sharrett, C. (2002). The End of the Road: David Cronenberg's "Crash" and the Fading of the West. Literature/Film Quarterly, 30(2), 126-132. jstor.org/stable/43797082

53   "Spectres of revolution" Mark Fisher, *k-punk*, 17 January 2010. k-punk.org/spectres-of-revolution/. Accessed 16 January 2025.

54   Georges Bataille. *Erotism: Death & Sensuality*. City Lights Books, 1986. 11.

55   Young, T. N. (2012). "Uses of the Erotic" for Teaching Queer Studies. Women's Studies Quarterly, 40(3/4), 301-305. jstor. org/stable/23333506

56   Cael M. Keegan, *Lana and Lilly Wachowski*. University of Illinois Press, 2018. p.47

57   "Reloaded clinch voted worst sex scene" Sean Clarke, *The Guardian*, 24 June 2003. theguardian.com/film/2003/jun/24/ news.seanclarke. Accessed 16 Jan 2025.

58   Mark Fisher. *Capitalist Realism*. Zer0 Books, 2009. p.15

59   Cael M. Keegan, *Lana and Lilly Wachowski*. University of Illinois Press, 2018. p.152

60   "Franco 'Bifo' Berardi on Flirting, Desire, Pleasure and Conspiration in the Age of Impotence" Giulia Crispiani, *Extra Extra Magazine*, 2020, extraextramagazine.com/talk/franco-bifo-berardi-on-flirting-desire-pleasure-and-conspiration-in-the-age-of-impotence/. Accessed 7 October 2024.

61   Ibid.

62   Linda Williams, *Screening Sex*. Duke University Press, 2008. p.141

63   Amia Srinivasan, *The Right to Sex*. Bloomsbury Publishing, 2021. p.51.

64   Kristen R. Ghodsee. *Why Women Have Better Sex Under Socialism*. Vintage Books, 2018. p.72.

65   Mulvey, L. (1975). Visual Pleasure and Narrative Cinema. Screen, 16(3), 6-18. doi.org/10.1093/screen/16.3.6

66   Ibid.

67   "What Women Want on "I Love Dick"" Emily Nussbaum, *The New Yorker*, 19 Jun 2017. newyorker.com/magazine/2017/06/26/what-women-want-on-i-love-dick. Accessed 29 October 2024.

68   "The Puritanical Eye: Hyper-Mediation, Sex on Film, and the Disavowal of Desire" Carlee Gomes, *Specchio Scuro*, 25 Nov 2023. specchioscuro.it/the-puritanical-eye-hyper-mediation-sex-on-film-and-the-disavowal-of-desire/. Accessed 16 January 2025.

69   Ann Snitow, Christine Stansell and Sharon Thompson, eds,

Powers of Desire: The Politics of Sexuality (Monthly Review Press, 1983), p.460. Quoted in Amia Srinivasan, *The Right to Sex*. Bloomsbury Publishing, 2021.

70   "Screening Female Desire: Bette Gordon's 'Variety' 35 Years On" Bette Gordon, Rebecca Liu, *Another Gaze*, 13 Feb 2019. anothergaze.com/screening-female-desire-bette-gordons-variety-35-years/. Accessed 8 November 2024.

71   Katherine Angel. *Tomorrow Sex Will Be Good Again: Women and Desire in the Age of Consent*. Verso Books, 2021. p.30

72   Amia Srinivasan, *The Right to Sex*. Bloomsbury Publishing, 2021. p.82

73   Ibid. p.84

74   Katherine Angel. *Tomorrow Sex Will Be Good Again: Women and Desire in the Age of Consent*. Verso Books, 2021. p.38-39

75   José Esteban Muñoz, *Cruising Utopia: The Then and There of Queer Futurity*. NYU Press, 2009.

76   "Uses of the Erotic: The Erotic as Power" From *Sister Outsider* by Audre Lorde. Crossing Press, 1987.

77   José Esteban Muñoz, *Cruising Utopia: The Then and There of Queer Futurity*. NYU Press, 2009. p.16.

78   "Thinking Sex: Notes for a Radical Theory of the Politics of Sexuality" Gayle S. Rubin in *Culture, Society and Sexuality: A Reader* edited by Richard Parker and Peter Aggleton. p.152.

79   José Esteban Muñoz, *Cruising Utopia: The Then and There of Queer Futurity*. NYU Press, 2009. p.48.

80   Ibid. p.1

81   "Levan Akin on the Impact of 'And Then We Danced'" Ed Meza, *Variety*, 19 August 2019. variety.com/2019/film/global/levan-akin-and-then-we-danced-1203305898/. Accessed 16 January 2025.

82   "Georgian March members trying to forcibly enter Amirani Cinema" *Interpressnews*, 8 November 2019. interpressnews.ge/en/article/104472-georgian-march-members-trying-to-forci-bly-enter-amirani-cinema. Accessed 16 January 2025.

83   "Georgian police vow to ensure peace amid threats voiced before premiere of film on gay love" *Agenda.ge*, 8 November 2019. agenda.ge/en/news/2019/3019#gsc.tab=0. Accessed 16 January 2025.

84 Sara Ahmed, *Queer Phenomenology: Orientations, Objects, Others*. Duke University Press, 2006. p.1

85 Ibid. p.15

86 Hu, J. (2021) Symmetry, Violence, and The Handmaiden's Queer Colonial Intimacies. Camera Obscura, 36 (2), 33–64. 10.1215/02705346-9052788

87 José Esteban Muñoz, *Cruising Utopia: The Then and There of Queer Futurity*. NYU Press, 2009. p.1.

88 Jones, A. (2009) Queer Heterotopias: Homonormativity and the Future of Queerness. interalia: a journal of queer studies. 4. 10.51897/interalia/PQBF4543.

89 "Isabel Sandoval on "Lingua Franca," Sex Scenes, and the Trans Female Gaze" Drew Burnett Gregory, *Autostraddle*, 28 August 2020. autostraddle.com/isabel-sandoval-on-lingua-franca-sex-scenes-and-the-trans-female-gaze/. Accessed 16 January 2025.

90 "John Cameron Mitchell's Erotic Romp 'Shortbus' Was the First and Last of Its Kind" Jude Dry, *IndieWire*, 26 January 2022. indiewire.com/features/general/john-cameron-mitchell-shortbus-interview-1234694076/. Accessed 16 January 2025.

91 Lauren Berlant and Lee Edelman, *Sex, or the Unbearable*. Duke University Press, 2014. p.8

92 José Esteban Muñoz, *Cruising Utopia: The Then and There of Queer Futurity*. NYU Press, 2009. p.32

93 Sara Ahmed, *Queer Phenomenology: Orientations, Objects, Others*. Duke University Press, 2006. p.103.

94 O'Brien, ME. (2019). To Abolish The Family. Endnotes, 5. p.390. endnotes.org.uk/articles/to-abolish-the-family.pdf.

95 Cael M. Keegan, *Lana and Lilly Wachowski*. University of Illinois Press, 2018. p.137

96 "Thinking Sex: Notes for a Radical Theory of the Politics of Sexuality" Gayle S. Rubin in *Culture, Society and Sexuality: A Reader* edited by Richard Parker and Peter Aggleton. p.143.

97 "Confronting the Abject: What Gaza Can Teach Us About the Struggles That Shape Our World" Tareq Baconi, *Lithub*, 5 June 2024. lithub.com/confronting-the-abject-what-gaza-can-teach-us-about-the-struggles-that-shape-our-world/. Accessed 16 January 2024.

98   "Queering the Map" queeringthemap.com. Accessed 16 January 2024.
99   Linda Williams, *Screening Sex*. Duke University Press, 2008. p.17

Acknowledgements

First of all, my utmost gratitude to Heather McDaid and Laura Jones-Rivera at 404 Ink for seeing potential in this book, and for brilliant stewardship of it from start to finish: it would not have been possible without your belief, patience, and all-around incredible dedication to what you do.

My (torrid) love affair with writing did not begin all that long ago, and I would not be here without every single editor who has championed me and given me opportunities I wouldn't have dared to dream of. Thank you especially to Douglas Greenwood, Ella Kemp, and David Jenkins for taking a chance on me right at the start. To Anahit Behrooz and Katie Goh, whose beautiful, world-making Inklings first inspired me to write *Revolutionary Desires* – thank you for making sure my earliest ideas cohered into more than errant rambles. Thanks also to Dr. Mihaela Mihai at the University of Edinburgh, whose guidance during my undergraduate dissertation helped plant the seeds of this book.

To my Take One Action colleagues Saoirse Amira Anis, Rachel Hamada, and Daisy Crooke, I am so grateful for all your morale-boosting and patience with me throughout this process – because of you, the radical power and connectivity of cinema is not just something I get to write about, but materially experience. For graciously reading excerpts of this book, a massive thank you to Rho Chung, doctor of gender (hell yeah), and the luminous Carlee Gomes. My warmest long-distance hug for Carlee and her other half of the Hit Factory podcast, Aaron Casias: you guys rock. I am so grateful to David Burns for teaching me to play the drums, which has kept me sane, and to Milli Hunter, for putting up with me writing in your flat.

Infinite love and gratitude to my family for their support, always, and thank you to my parents for being only slightly quizzical and mostly chill about their kid writing a book about sex scenes. Many thanks to Cecilia Bondestam, who has seen me go from "it's so over" to "we're so back" more times than anyone else. To Daisy (again), for endless sunshine and making it possible for me to do what I love. To Anahit (again), it is a thrill that the best and most inspiring writer I will ever know is also my friend. To Janine Awunyo, a light of my life: your warmth, humour, kindness, and belief in the fight lifts me up all the time.

And to Louis Cammell, I love you like in the movies: so much that it makes me love the world even more than I thought possible. Thank you for every single day. Thank you for showing me what it means.

About the Author

Xuanlin Tham is a writer and curator based in Edinburgh. They programme for Take One Action, an arts organisation harnessing the transformative power of film and storytelling for collective change in Scotland and beyond. Their writing has been published in British *GQ*, *i-D*, *Little White Lies*, *AnOther Magazine*, and *The Skinny*, among others, covering film, culture, and sometimes sports.

About the Inklings series

This book is part of 404 Ink's Inkling series which presents big ideas in pocket-sized books.

They are all available at 404ink.com/shop.

If you enjoyed this book, you may also enjoy these titles in the series:

Solemates – Adam Zmith

Solemates brings to light the history of this peculiarly popular kink. From Tarantino films to Bible stories, from Renaissance paintings to OnlyFans, Solemates is the rich and messy tale of our obsession with everything below the ankle, and what it reveals about how we view our bodies and our sex lives.

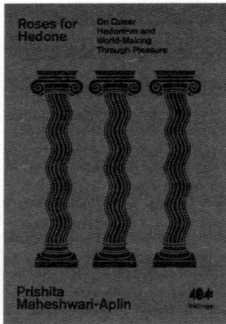

Roses for Hedone – Prishita Maheshwari-Aplin

As we face ongoing and new challenges to creating a fairer world, let us borrow from the Ancient Greeks' understanding of love's multiplicity to explore queer hedonism not as a momentary phenomenon, but rather a transformational route through which we can learn from our past, connect in the present, and look towards the future with hope – together.

Look, Don't Touch – layla-roxanne hill & Francesca Sobande

Look, Don't Touch journeys through the music of feeling, "self-help" social media, the power of public signage, and more to call for a move away from the language of "okayness", and a move towards collectively uplifting forms of anger, agitation, love, solidarity, release, and ultimately, *feeling*.